STAR WARS®

Acknowledgments

We couldn't have done this book without the generous collaboration of George Lucas, Rick McCallum, and the entire cast and crew of *Star Wars*: Episode I *The Phantom Menace*. Our gratitude to the following who also made this book possible (in alphabetical order):

At Lucasfilm: Matthew Azeveda, Jane Bay, Mark Becker, Chris Butler, Scott Carter, Jeanne Cole, Cara Evangelista, Justin Graham, Lynne Hale, Ardees Jundis, Allan Kausch, Halina Krukowski, Gillian Libbert, Anne Merrifield, Tina Mills, Rachel Milstein, Janet Nielsen, Howard Roffman, Karen Rose, Sue Rostoni, Jon Shenk, Janet Talamantes, Blake Tucker, Jim Ward, Patty Weichel, Lucy Wilson.

At ILM: Fay David, Christine Owens, Ellen Pasternack, Nagisa Yamamoto.

At Ballantine Books: Min Choi, Fred Dodnick, Alexandra Krijgsman, Cathy Repetti, Dave Stevenson; and Sylvain Michaelis of Michaelis/Carpelis Design Associates, Inc.

And: Kelly Bush, Kate Campbell, Janey Richardson.

In addition, Laurent Bouzereau wishes to thank his parents, Daniel and Micheline; his sisters, Cécile and Géraldine; Valérie Young; Colleen Benn; Marty Cohen; and his agent, Kay McCauley. Jody Duncan extends her love and gratitude to Caitlin Shannon and Larry Deckel.

Introduction

"It's been a long time comin'," as the song goes.

For sixteen years, ever since the release of *Return of the Jedi*, the final feature in the *Star Wars* trilogy, the world had waited for the promised prequel episodes that would explain how it all began. Occasionally, rumors would spread among fans and within the media: "Finally, there is a script." "Casting has begun." But such rumors would quickly dead-end, and the long, long wait would continue.

The audience's appetite for the new films were only whetted by the release of *Star Wars Special Edition* in 1997, the twentieth anniversary of a film that had become as much a part of American culture as any in history. Writer/director George Lucas's classic tale of good versus evil, set "a long time ago in a galaxy far, far away" sparked a renaissance of the science fiction movie genre and revolutionized visual effects technology. An unprecedented amount of merchandise was generated. Books and magazines devoted to *Star Wars* were published. Acting careers were made. An empire called Lucasfilm was built, as was the venerable Industrial Light & Magic. Skywalker Ranch grew out of the rolling green hills of Marin County. And George Lucas became a bona fide icon before reaching his thirty-fifth birthday.

During the development of the original *Star Wars*, Lucas had realized that the story he had in mind was too broad, too sweeping for a single movie; and so he split the story line into a series of movies, deciding to begin with the fourth episode, *Star Wars: A New Hope*, and hoping that the film would be successful enough to warrant the making of the following chapters. Smart money said that it would not: Lucas was a young director, and the movie itself was a throwback to a style and subject matter that had long gone out of fashion. Nobody, not even Lucas himself, suspected that *Star Wars* would be a phenomenon.

But a phenomenon it was. *Star Wars* fever was only heightened with the extraordinarily successful releases of *The Empire Strikes Back* in 1980 and *Return of the Jedi* in 1983. Fourteen years later, the overwhelming response to the *Special Editions* of all three films by a whole new generation of moviegoers proved that Lucas's space opera was as timely and relevant in the late nineties as it had been in the seventies and eighties.

We wanted more.

Finally, we're getting it. For nearly five years, Lucas and producer Rick McCallum worked together to bring the long-awaited

Sixteen years after the release of the last *Star Wars* installment, writer/director George Lucas delivered the long-promised Episode I *The Phantom Menace.*

Young actress Natalie Portman took on the dual role of Padmé the hand-maiden and Queen Amidala.

Just as he had done in the original trilogy, Lucas constructed Episode I to illustrate a number of themes, subtly woven through a plot-intensive narrative. "Duality is one of the main themes of the film," Lucas revealed. "There is duality in the character of the Queen, who trades places with one of her handmaidens, Padmé, as a decoy. Duality is also present in the characters of Obi-Wan and Qui-Gon. In the beginning, Obi-Wan is at odds with Qui-Gon, who rebels against the Jedi rules. But by the end of the film, he has *become* Qui-Gon by taking on his rebellious personality and his responsibilities."

Another major theme was the notion of symbiotic relationships—life forms living together for mutual advantage. That theme was most deftly illuminated through the character of Anakin. In the story, it is suggested that Anakin was conceived by midi-chlorians—living organisms found in cells, through which people are able to communicate with the Force. A symbiotic relationship exists between Anakin—or any person with whom the Force is strong—and the midi-

chlorians: the former draws strength, wisdom and insight from the midi-chlorians, while the midi-chlorians rely on such beings to sustain life.

"The midi-chlorians have brought Anakin into being as 'the chosen one' who will balance the universe," Lucas elaborated. "The mystery around that theory is that we don't know yet whether the chosen one is a good or a bad person. He is to bring balance to the Force; but at this point, we don't know what side of the Force needs to be balanced out."

Balance would also emerge as a recurring theme in the story. "The overriding philosophy in Episode I—and in all the *Star Wars* movies, for that matter—is the balance between good and evil. The Force itself breaks into two sides: the living Force and a greater, cosmic Force. The living Force makes you sensitive to other living things, makes you intuitive, and allows you to read other people's minds, et cetera. But the greater Force has to do with destiny. In working with the Force, you can find your destiny and you can choose to either follow it, or not."

The search for balance was a theme that governed the writing process, as well, as Lucas struggled to orchestrate a story with many characters, plots, and subplots. "*Star Wars* was a balance of many characters and many stories," Lucas said. "And each subsequent *Star Wars* movie had more characters and stories than the previous one. Writing a story is very practical—in order to construct scenes, you need to have interaction, people talking to one another, otherwise you wouldn't have drama. Anakin needed to have a mother, Obi-Wan needed a Master, Darth Sidious needed an apprentice. Everyone has to have somebody who influences them."

Both themes and characters emerged from an overall story that would feature five plots going on simultaneously, one leading to another. The basic story underlying all the others is how Senator Palpatine becomes the chancellor of the Republic. "Everything else

The Force is unusually strong in young Anakin Skywalker.

revolves around that story line," Lucas said. "The second plot is about the Trade Federation trying to gain control over an out-of-the-way planet ruled by a young Queen, and how that Queen repulses the invaders. That story line precipitates the third, which is the chancellor sending Jedi Knights to try and negotiate peace, and the way in which those Knights get intertwined in the political arena of this invasion. We are introduced to Qui-Gon, who is very independent, always testing the rules. And we meet young Obi-Wan, who is constantly frustrated by his Master's refusal to go along with the program. The fourth story line involves young Anakin Skywalker and how he becomes a Jedi. That leads to the fifth story point, which deals with the rise of the Sith Lords, and the Jedi concerns about the fact that they've been resurrected after a thousand years."

Before it was completed, Lucas would revise those basic stories and the screenplay as a whole nearly twenty times. But even then, the story was not set in stone. Lucas would continue to revise and rework the narrative through production and, most profoundly, during the editing stage.

As Lucas began to wrestle with the screenplay, Rick McCallum initiated preparations for the production that would continue for two full years before cameras rolled. McCallum had been Lucas's collaborator ever since 1990, when he produced the feature film *Radioland Murders* and, later, the critically acclaimed television series *The Young Indiana Jones Chronicles*. That series—filmed over a period of three years, in thirty countries—had received twenty-five Emmy nominations and had won eleven, as well as a 1993 Golden Globe nomination for best dramatic series.

done by Ralph McQuarrie for *Return of the Jedi*, but never used. McQuarrie's designs were also instrumental in developing the look of Coruscant. "George wanted to push Ralph's ideas even further for this movie," Chiang said. "He wanted to show a variety of vistas and different areas of the planet. It was a relatively simple task to come up with the Coruscant designs, since Ralph had already established a style. All I did was take his vision and expand on it a little."

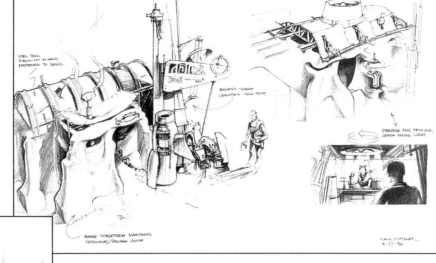

Distinctive styles were developed for the three main buildings featured in the Coruscant sequence: the senate building, Palpatine's quarters, and the Jedi Council chamber. "When audiences saw any one of those sets, George wanted them to know that the action had moved to an entirely different part of the planet. In many ways, it was like designing three different cities in three separate worlds."

For the senate building, Chiang expanded on McQuarrie's original supermetropolis design. "I just pushed the scale, the texture, and the composition of Ralph's drawings," Chiang explained. "I opted for a sleek, modern vision, incorporating more steel, glass, and weird plastic materials. The forms also became a little cleaner and more streamlined." The senate chamber itself would feature floating platforms—originally conceived as spectator platforms for the Podrace

sequence. "George was looking for something visually interesting and dynamic for the senate chamber scene, so we pulled the unused idea of the flying platforms from Tatooine, put them on Coruscant, and refined the designs to make them big, bowl-shaped enclosures."

In contrast to the corporate coldness of the senate building, the Jedi Council architecture was designed to suggest a place of worship, a place that was both religious and monumental. For reference, Chiang took pictures of monuments from various cultures,

Concept drawings of the Mos Espa Arena (left) and street scenes (top and bottom)

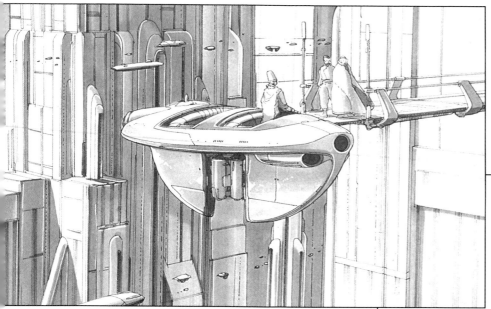

animals live in their environments, and how they interact with each other," Whitlatch commented, "and so I was able to come up with new species that seemed plausible within the world of *Star Wars*."

Whitlatch started by building up a photographic library of real animals, which she reviewed with Lucas. The director would then

A variety of concepts were drawn and considered before a final look was established for the planet Coruscant.

then exaggerated their shapes and heights in his drawings.

Creatures and species indigenous to each of these cities and planets also had to be designed. Although the entire art department would have a hand in such designs, Terryl Whitlatch's background in zoology and anatomy made the artist particularly well suited to the task of designing Episode I's characters. "I have an understanding of how

suggest that a specific feature of one animal be combined with a feature of another, resulting in a hybrid that would form the basis for an entirely new species. One character born in such a manner was Watto, the flying, trunked, pot-bellied junk shop dealer who loses his slave Anakin to Qui-Gon in the Podrace. "I had done a portrait of an ugly, cherub-type thing with tiny wings," Whitlatch recalled. "George saw it, suggested we give it duck feet, and Watto was born."

In some cases, a creature designed for one environment would be moved into another, per Lucas's request. The two-legged kaadu, for example, were initially intended for Tatooine, as the creatures used to pull Anakin's Podracer engines toward the race arena. Eventually, however, the kaadu were drafted for the Otoh Gunga sequence.

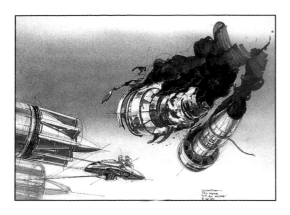

A spade was the inspiration for the attack tanks. "I took that basic shovel shape, put a big turret on it, and made a flying vehicle that looked as if it was made of iron."

The small flying vehicles used by the droid army—called STAPs—were designed as a variation on the speeder bikes from *Return of the Jedi*. Chiang toyed with the design until he came up with a kind of Jet Ski vehicle. "Going back to nature," Chiang elaborated, "I took the idea of the hummingbird and applied it to the STAPs, adding tiny wings down below and making the head itself very sleek." Streamlined versions of

vehicle were the hovering tanks dispatched by the Neimoidians for the invasion and final battle on Naboo. Tanks were divided into two types: the multi-troop transports (MTTs) that would deliver battle and destroyer droids to the battleground, and AATs, the armored attack tanks. "We felt that the MTT should reflect the fact that the droids had animalistic features," Chiang observed, "and I immediately imagined a charging elephant. The cockpit of the vehicle resembles the head of an elephant, the big trunk area is the body, and the side arms with guns are the tusks."

Left: Renderings for the Podrace sequence included a depiction of an exploding Podracer, an eopie pulling a Podracer engine, and the racers at the starting grid. **Below:** Orthographic renderings of various Podracers. **Opposite page:** Concept drawings of the Trade Federation multi-troop transports (MTTs).

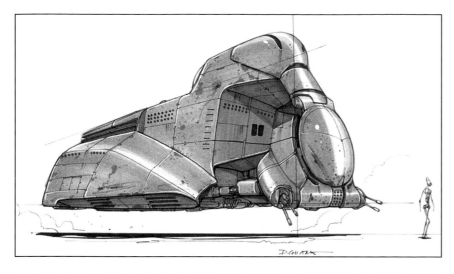

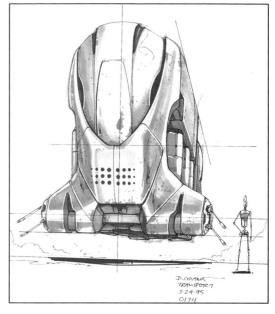

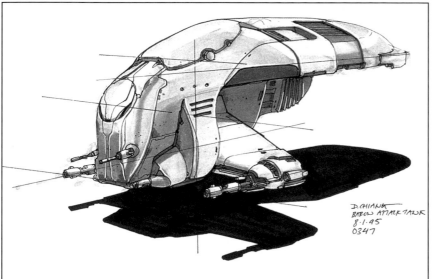

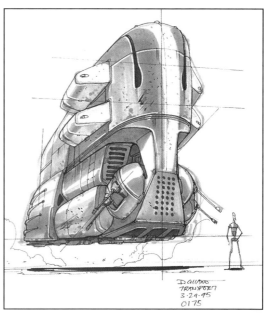

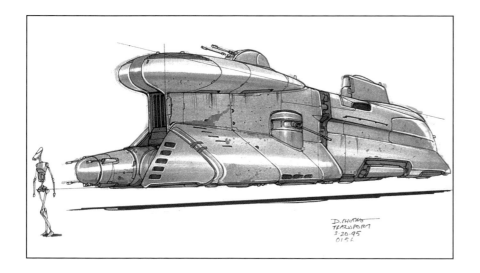

Luke Skywalker's landspeeder from the first *Star Wars* would also be seen on Naboo.

In the story, Obi-Wan, Qui-Gon, and Jar Jar would pilot a submarine through the watery core of Naboo. After exploring everything from traditional sub designs to art nouveau influences, Chiang based the sub on a squid. "The propellers are very squidlike and form an elegant tail," Chiang explained.

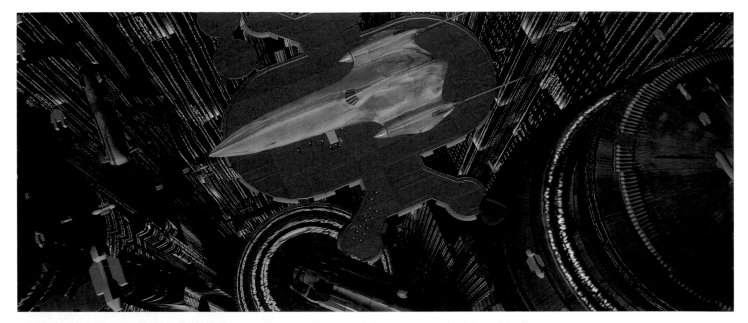

The animatics provided crucial reference on the set, enabling Lucas to see exactly how each shot needed to be set up, and giving the actors—who would often be working against bluescreen or with CG characters absent from the live-action scene— a sense of how the action would play out once all the elements were combined in the final film.
Above: The Queen's transport on a landing pad on Coruscant.
Left: Darth Maul's Sith infiltrator in the Tatooine desert.

the Podrace very early on," McCallum commented. "He could look at the basic concept for the race, then start playing with it—'I'd like to zoom back here; I want this to be a fifty-millimeter lens; I'd like it to be two frames shorter at the head and six frames longer at the tail'—and boom, it would be there in the animatic. We did that, shot by shot. It was slow at first. For the first couple of weeks, we were only producing maybe three seconds per week. But then David got more sophisticated, we hired another couple of people to work with him, and it really

started to go. We were pumping out a minute's worth of film per week. Eventually, all of those shots were cut into a sequence— and suddenly, we had the Podrace, all there, all worked out. It was a fantastic tool."

In a similar fashion, animatics were created for virtually every sequence in the film. They were ultimately not only used as a pre-visualization tool, they were also used on the set. Played on a monitor set up next to the director, the animatics provided crucial reference in setting up shots. The animatics continued to prove useful in the editing

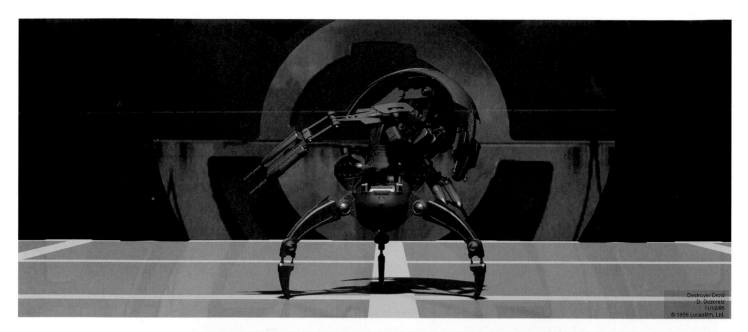

Destroyer Droid
D. Dozoretz
11/12/96
© 1996 Lucasfilm, Ltd.

Animatics were equally useful in the editing phase to provide temporary visuals that could be cut into the as yet unfinished film, giving the filmmakers a sense of the movie's flow and rhythm.
Above: A destroyer droid animatic.
Right: Battle droids.

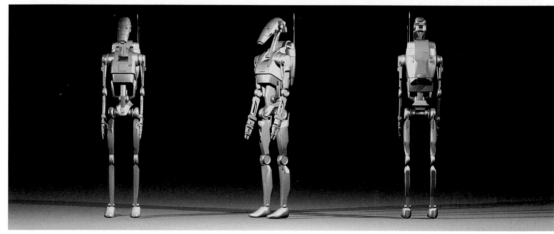

phase—instead of sterile "scene missing" cards inserted into a rough cut of the film to mark shots that had not yet been completed by the effects team, the animatic for that scene was cut in, creating a sense of continuity in even the roughest cuts of the movie.

All the exacting attention paid to writing the screenplay, to designing sets and aliens and costumes, to choreographing dynamic action sequences—all of that would be for naught if the right actors could not be found. Fortunately, there was no dearth of

actors willing and even eager to be a part of the first *Star Wars* movie in sixteen years. Still, the casting of Episode I—initiated in early 1995—was a long and arduous process, complicated considerably by the fact that some key roles would have to be cast to match actors who had been featured in *Episodes IV*, *V*, and *VI*. Lucas didn't simply need a good young actor to portray Obi-Wan Kenobi, for example; he needed a good young actor who also bore some resemblance to Alec Guinness, the actor who had portrayed the older version of the character in

the first *Star Wars*. He didn't simply need a child actor to play Anakin Skywalker; he needed a child actor with enough mystery and complexity to play a boy who would grow up to be Darth Vader, and who could be convincing as a child of extraordinary gifts.

The development phase of the movie had been progressing for about a year when Rick McCallum met casting director Robin Gurland. Gurland had worked out of San Francisco and had cast a number of films in the area. Having already decided that he didn't want to go with one of the large, well-known casting organizations, McCallum felt that, in Gurland, he had found the right casting director for Episode I. A year after their first meeting, he hired her for the job. "I gave her the opportunity to start very early on," McCallum recalled, "and to stay on the film throughout the whole process. It was an incredible journey. She was the perfect person—so full of energy, and so focused and dedicated."

Gurland would see actors in seven different countries over a period of two years in her quest to fill the key roles. American

actors, British actors, stars, and unknowns all came to the table equally. The only criteria was whether the actor was right for the material. "It was always about who was right for the role," Gurland attested. "If it was someone the public knew, fine. If it wasn't, that was just as well. As a casting director, it gave me an unbelievable sense of freedom to know that I was not constrained by a studio or public recognition quotients."

Top: A computer-generated view of the Jedi Temple. Above: Casting director Robin Gurland on the set at Leavesden Studios with George Lucas and Rick McCallum.

A low-resolution computer-generated animatic of the senate building on Coruscant.

Slowly and meticulously, Gurland began to assemble lists of names, accompanied by photographs. "The characters were very well defined," Gurland commented, "and I could immediately visualize them. There was no ambiguity, which made it very easy to understand what George wanted in these characters." After two years, Gurland had narrowed the list down to a few key candidates, all of whom would be brought in to meet George Lucas.

Coming into the casting process with no preconceived notions, Lucas considered the actors with an open mind, sitting and talking to them in a very casual, pressure-free atmosphere. "We would meet with the actors," Gurland recalled, "but we never showed them the script—which surprised most of them. They would just come in and chat with George, Rick, and myself about anything and everything—politics, religion, theater. In fact, we talked about everything *except* for *Star Wars*. George was looking to find out who the person was and how he or

she matched the vision he had of a particular character."

"I was looking for specific personality traits and charismatic qualities," Lucas added. "I wanted to get a feeling about their natures by the way they carried themselves. Since I was most interested in the ensemble, and how the characters would play against each other, I was mainly trying to find the right pieces of the overall puzzle."

One piece of the puzzle that fell sublimely into place was Liam Neeson, cast in the pivotal role of Jedi Master Qui-Gon Jinn. Because the character had been described as a man in his sixties in the script, Gurland had looked initially for older actors; and yet, inexplicably, Irish-born Liam Neeson—a much younger man—kept appearing on her A-list. Certainly Neeson had the credentials. He had been nominated for an Academy Award for his title role in *Schindler's List*; and had since become an international motion picture star through his lead performances in films such as *Rob Roy*, *Michael Collins*, and

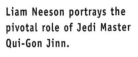
Liam Neeson portrays the pivotal role of Jedi Master Qui-Gon Jinn.

Les Misérables. But, in addition to the age issue, the filmmakers had envisioned an American actor in the role of Qui-Gon.

"I kept putting Liam's name down," Gurland said, "even though I was looking for an American actor. He had so many of the right elements for the character. He had that mythic hero quality and a strong physical and spiritual presence." In addition, the filmmakers began to consider the fact that a man of Neeson's age, as opposed to an older actor, would be more plausible as a Jedi warrior.

A fortuitous chain of events would lead to Neeson's casting. True to his usual style when interviewing actors, Lucas avoided the topic of *Star Wars* altogether. "We actually talked about kids," Neeson recalled. "George is a family man, and I have two little boys—and that's what we talked about. The only time *Star Wars* came up was as I was leaving, when I said to him, 'For what it's worth, George, I would love to be a part of this film.'"

Soon thereafter, Rick McCallum was in negotiations with Neeson, and the actor was cast. "Liam Neeson *is* a master Jedi," George Lucas commented, "the center of the movie—just like Alec Guinness was in the first movie. When you start to cast a character like this, you think, 'Where are we going to find another Alec Guinness? Where are we going to find someone with that kind of nobility, that kind of strength, and that kind of center?' Liam was the guy who could do it. There *wasn't* anybody else who could do it. And when we saw him in the part, it was like, 'Of course. It's a natural.' He had the presence we needed. He was tall and very strong, with a powerful nature. And like Alec Guinness in the original movies, he was an actor that other members of the cast looked up to."

For his part, Neeson thought of Qui-Gon as a timeless sort of soul. "He is almost like a monk," Neeson observed, "an old-time warrior who is wise and quite philosophical, yet very skilled in martial arts. He has incredible confidence, as well as a magical quality that enables him to see into the future. He is not really a rebel, but he has his own code." To prepare for the role, Neeson not only watched all three original *Star Wars* movies again, he also reviewed *The Seven Samurai*. "I wanted to get a feel for the depiction of characters with great dignity and courage."

Cast in the role of Qui-Gon's pupil, Obi-Wan Kenobi, was Ewan McGregor, best known for his performance in *Trainspotting*. When McGregor first met with Robin Gurland, his wife was pregnant; but their baby daughter would be a year old before the actor was officially cast as Obi-Wan.

The challenge of casting the role was to find an actor who would be believable as a young Alec Guinness. Armed with pictures of Guinness as a young man, Gurland selected fifty actors who had potential. "I asked

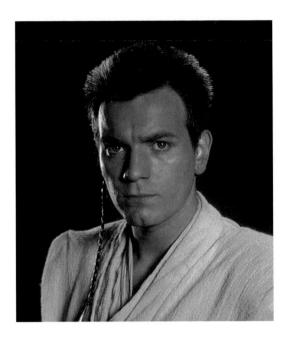

Robin to do a composite split screen on tape," McCallum said, "so that we could run pictures of those fifty actors against those of young Alec Guinness." Among those who fared well in the comparison was Ewan McGregor.

"Ewan had the same kind of physique as Alec," Gurland commented. "And then, the first time I met him, it was evident that he could play the character. There was no doubt in my mind."

McGregor's first meeting with George Lucas—like Liam Neeson's—consisted of easy conversation about children, and then moved to talk of *Star Wars*. "He mentioned how long it had taken him to shoot the first trilogy," McGregor said, "and how old his kids would be when he completed the new three films." Through that conversation, Lucas learned that Denis Lawson, who had played the character of Wedge in all three *Star Wars* films, was McGregor's uncle. In a sense, through that familial connection, McGregor had lived with *Star Wars* his whole life, and had grown up fascinated with the trilogy.

By the end of the meeting, Lucas was satisfied that he had found his Obi-Wan. "Ewan McGregor is the young Turk of the European film community," Lucas observed. "He is an extremely strong actor and he has the energy, the grace, and the enthusiasm to play a young Obi-Wan Kenobi."

While many of the actors would go through physical training to prepare for the filming of Episode I, McGregor, alone, was faced with the additional challenge of training his voice and learning a dialect that would more closely resemble Alec Guinness's from the previous movies. "There was something very paternal and calming about his voice," McGregor explained. "I had to undergo a lot of dialogue coaching to get a younger-sounding version of that voice. It was quite tricky."

No role was more difficult to cast than that of nine-year-old Anakin Skywalker—and both Robin Gurland and the filmmakers had known from the beginning that it would be. The child cast in the role would have to be a good actor, obviously, but would also have to possess an intelligence and even a dignity that would make him believable as "the chosen one." "Children's roles are usually not so complex," Gurland observed, "because there are very few child actors who have that range of emotion."

Rather than set up open casting calls—as is customary in the casting of young children—Gurland met with child actors one by one, in part to ensure secrecy. Before it was over, Gurland would meet and/or audition close to three thousand children. Early in the process, she met a five-year-old named Jake Lloyd. "He was too young at the time," Gurland recalled, "but even then there was something magical about him, a quality that was perfect for Anakin. So I kept him in mind, thinking that by the time we started

Jake Lloyd as Anakin Skywalker and Natalie Portman as Padmé.

shooting, he might be the right age." Two years later, the role still had not been cast—and Jake Lloyd, as little boys tend to do, had grown. "Suddenly, he was seven years old; so I sent him for a screen test with two other boys at Skywalker Ranch." Lloyd tested well, and he was cast as Anakin Skywalker.

"Jake Lloyd was a natural," Lucas said. "He was bouncy, cheerful, everything we wanted. He reminded me of a young Luke Skywalker; and that was good because he had to embody the same presence that Luke had in the first film."

Although Lloyd had already appeared in *Unhook the Stars* and *Jingle All the Way* by the time he was cast in Episode I, he was anything but unaffected by the news of his casting. "Robin called my agent and asked, 'How would Jake and his parents like to spend the summer in London?'" Lloyd recalled. "And when I found out, I screamed, 'Oooaaah!' It was very cool. I started bawling, I was so happy! Now everyone will know who is behind the mask of Darth Vader!"

Cast in the dual role of fourteen-year-old Queen Amidala and her handmaiden Padmé was sixteen-year-old Natalie Portman.

Portman was already a seasoned professional, having played roles in *The Professional, Everyone Says I Love You, Mars Attacks!, Beautiful Girls*, and *Heat*. In addition to her film work, Portman was scheduled to make her Broadway debut in the title role of *The Diary of Anne Frank*.

Robin Gurland thought of the wise-beyond-her-years, graceful Portman the moment George Lucas first described the character of the Queen to her. After meeting with Gurland and then Lucas, Portman was offered the role. "Natalie is very strong and mature for her age," Lucas noted. "And like Carrie Fisher, she had the personality to carry the role of a leader."

The challenge of playing two roles in one film was one that appealed to the young actress. "It was exciting for me because I really had to make the two characters different so that it wouldn't spoil the surprise when Padmé's true identity is revealed," Portman said. "I did two different voices and tried to move differently, as well. Padmé was more physical than the Queen, for example." Portman developed two different dialects as well, through the help of dialect coach Joan

Ian McDiarmid as Senator Palpatine and Pernilla August as Shmi, Anakin's mother.

Washington. "For Padmé, I played with my own voice; but when I was the Queen, we made up an accent that was kind of like the fake British accent people did back in the days of old-school Hollywood."

The only on-screen actor from the first trilogy to reprise his role in Episode I was Ian McDiarmid, who would return—without old-age makeup—as a younger version of Palpatine, the aging Emperor seen in *Return of the Jedi*. Episode I picks up the story with Palpatine as a senator of the Republic who is already implementing plans that will lead to the formation of his empire. In addition to his work in *Return of the Jedi*, McDiarmid had enjoyed a career on stage and in feature films such as *Dragonslayer, Gorky Park, Dirty Rotten Scoundrels*, and *Restoration* before joining the Episode I cast. McDiarmid also runs the prestigious Almeida Theatre in London.

For the role of Shmi, Anakin's mother, Lucas envisioned a warm but solid woman. "She is caught in a struggle," Lucas commented. "She loves her son, but she wants a better life for him and has to let him go. I wanted to be able to read that struggle on

her face." Pernilla August, the Swedish actress who would ultimately play the role, had starred in two episodes of *The Young Indiana Jones Chronicles* and was therefore familiar to both Lucas and Rick McCallum.

"We were initially thinking of someone British and older for Shmi," McCallum stated, "but the moment you looked at Pernilla, you could see that she had the right qualities for the character. We brought her in to meet George and do a screen test, and it all happened from there."

August herself had some concerns, which she expressed in her meeting with Lucas. "I told him that I was worried about my Swedish accent," August related, "and he said to me, 'Don't worry about it; Shmi comes from a Swedish galaxy!' From that point on, I had complete confidence, because I knew George had confidence in me."

One of the film's most familiar faces is Samuel L. Jackson, who appears as the Jedi Council member Mace Windu. Jackson gained stature as a film actor through his performances in *Pulp Fiction, Jackie Brown, Sphere*, and *Jungle Fever*. The Jedi role in Episode I was more modest than any he'd played in a

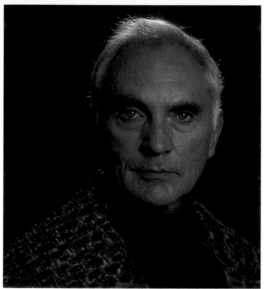

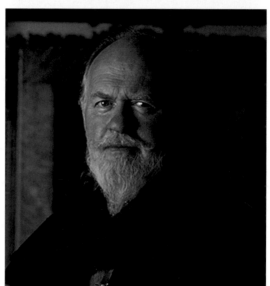

Clockwise from top left:
Samuel L. Jackson (Mace
Windu), Ray Park (Darth
Maul), Oliver Ford Davies
(Sio Bibble), and Terence
Stamp (Chancellor Valorum).

long time—yet the actor actively petitioned for the role. While on a talk show in London publicizing his new film—and knowing that the production was being filmed nearby—Jackson let it be known that he would do anything to be in the new *Star Wars* movie. Gurland heard about Jackson's on-air comments the next day, and immediately got in touch with his agent. "Sam's approach was so genuine," Gurland remarked. "But he also happened to be right for the character—

although the role is definitely different from the other parts he's played."

"I'm a huge fan of the *Star Wars* saga," Jackson said, "and it was an experience I really wanted. When I was on that talk show, I guess I saw an opportunity—so I just said it. 'I'd really like to be in the new *Star Wars*.' And it was the truth."

Stuntman Ray Park was initially cast as Darth Maul primarily because of his swordsmanship and martial arts skills—both of

48

Clockwise from top left: Ralph Brown (Ric Olié), Hugh Quarshie (Captain Panaka), Anthony Daniels (C-3PO), and Kenny Baker (R2-D2).

which would prove valuable in the long lightsaber battle between Darth Maul, Qui-Gon, and Obi-Wan. But after testing him in makeup and costume, the filmmakers realized that the actor embodied *all* of the qualities of the Sith Lord.

Gurland assembled an impressive list of talents for other supporting roles, as well. "It was thrilling for me to be able to cast excellent actors such as Terence Stamp, who plays Chancellor Valorum, Ralph Brown as

the Naboo pilot Ric Olié, Oliver Ford Davies as Sio Bibble, and Hugh Quarshie as Captain Panaka," Gurland said. "These were smaller roles that, typically, they wouldn't do. But because they all wanted to work with George, everyone said, 'Absolutely! No question!' We also brought back Anthony Daniels as See-Threepio and Kenny Baker as Artoo-Detoo. And to play Wald, one of Anakin's friends, George wanted Warwick Davis who, ever since *Return of the Jedi* and then

Willow, has become part of the family."

In addition to the on-screen roles, Episode I would boast a number of prominent characters realized entirely through computer animation; yet those characters still needed vocal performances to bring them to life. In the case of Jar Jar, who would play a major role in the movie, not only vocal talent was needed. Lucas also wanted an actor on the set who would interact with the other actors, develop the character, and provide invaluable reference to the CG team when it came time to animate the Gungan.

It was a task actor Ahmed Best was eager to take on. Gurland discovered the actor in a performance of *Stomp*, the percussion theater show. "George knew he wanted a bumbling type," Gurland said, "but there wasn't any definitive description of Jar Jar, other than he was high energy, comedic, and somewhat improvisational. So when I went to this performance of *Stomp* and saw Ahmed moving his arms with a kitchen sink wrapped around his neck, I immediately thought, 'He's Jar Jar!'" Without explaining her purpose, Gurland arranged a meeting with Best,

which she videotaped. "I asked him to do a bit of improv for me. I told him to imagine himself as a very gangly being who is eating a clam—and I saw Jar Jar come to life." Gurland rushed the tape to Lucas and McCallum, who were both similarly impressed.

"Originally," Lucas recalled, "we wanted Ahmed because he was so good at using his body, and we were looking for someone who could perform unique body movements. But then I had him do the dialogue, and I liked

Warwick Davis in costume as a Rodian portrays Anakin's friend Wald. Top right and above: Although Jar Jar would be realized entirely through computer graphics, actor Ahmed Best provided both the character's vocal performance and an on-set characterization that provided reference for the animators. Best was fitted with a costume to ensure correct eyelines and give the CG team reference as to how light would play on Jar Jar's skin and clothing.

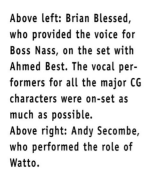

Above left: Brian Blessed, who provided the voice for Boss Nass, on the set with Ahmed Best. The vocal performers for all the major CG characters were on-set as much as possible.
Above right: Andy Secombe, who performed the role of Watto.

what he did there, as well. As soon as we started shooting, it became obvious that he believed in his lines and in his character. He found the meaning behind the character."

Jar Jar was perhaps the most risky character of all—not only because he would be entirely computer generated, but because he was the first truly comedic character ever to inhabit a *Star Wars* movie. "George told me that we were really going out on a limb," Best recalled. "See-Threepio was funny, but in a very formal, dry way. And Chewbacca got some laughs, but he was basically just a big bouncer for the *Millennium Falcon*. Jar Jar was the first outright comic character." Despite the fact that his face and body would not be seen in the final film, Best was honored to create the character. "The original *Star Wars* was the first movie I ever saw. And, as a kid, I had the *Star Wars* bed sheets, pillow cases, curtains, *and* the action figures!"

Other vocal talents were hired on the basis of tapes gathered by Gurland and reviewed by Lucas. "For the voices of the characters," Lucas said, "I had a rough idea of what they should sound like. But sometimes, after listening to one of Robin's

tapes, I would change my mind and go in a completely different direction. It was an evolving process."

While, typically, voice talent would not be hired until postproduction, Lucas cast the voices of CG characters such as Watto and the Gungan Boss Nass before cameras rolled, so that those actors could be on the set, relating to other actors in the scenes. In addition, as was the case with Jar Jar, the on-set performances would provide the CG animators with excellent reference when it came time to animate the characters.

In looking for the voice of Boss Nass, Gurland took her cues from the character's appearance, as drawn by the art department. "Boss Nass was bigger than life," Gurland recalled, "and seemed to have a kind of bravado. I had brought in actor Brian Blessed for a general meeting with George, and he blew us away—so I knew I wanted him involved, but I didn't know yet where. He was so grand and commanding! When Boss Nass had to be cast three or four months later, Brian immediately came to mind."

Another actor who would perform on-set was Andy Secombe, who provided the voice for Watto. Stand-up comedians Greg Proops and Scott Capurro were also pegged for the two-headed Podrace announcer, who would be realized through computer animation.

With the cast assembled, George Lucas gathered the actors together for a complete reading of the script shortly before the start of filming. The reading allowed the actors to familiarize themselves with their roles and the overall story line, and also served to break the ice between people who, in most cases, had never met before this day. "Usually when you go through the first reading," Lucas commented, "you expect to have a lot of hurdles to overcome. But that reading went great. Everybody sailed right through it. Everything worked. Because we had terrific actors, the dialogue sounded plausible and realistic."

Episode I had been in preproduction for nearly two years as the summer of 1996 rolled around. The screenplay was completed, more or less; thousands of designs had been realized; and a majority of the roles had been cast. Now, with the shoot less than a year away, the filmmakers turned their

attention to the actual building of the production elements. "George had developed every single aspect of the film in his mind and on paper," Rick McCallum noted, "but now, sets needed to be built, creatures had to be made, costumes needed to be sewn. The time had come to make all those ideas a reality."

In August 1996, Gavin Bocquet and a small art department arrived at Leavesden Studios in London to do just that. Leavesden was not, in fact, a "studio" at all, but rather

Above: Stand-up comedians Greg Proops and Scott Capurro performed in elaborate makeup as the two-headed Podrace announcer, providing crucial reference for the CG team that eventually realized the character. Below: Leavesden Studios, outside of London, was leased by the production for two and a half years, allowing Lucas and McCallum a measure of flexibility in the shooting schedule.

Above: A total of sixty-some sets were built for the production, the majority being interiors erected at Leavesden Studios.
Right: The entire build was orchestrated by production designer Gavin Bocquet.

photography had wrapped—an important aspect of the *Young Indy*–style filmmaking structure McCallum and Lucas intended to implement for Episode I. Bocquet, whose job it would be to transform the cavernous soundstages into movie sets, observed, "Normally studios expect to clear out one group of sets and get the next film right in to pay the rent. It was a great advantage to Lucasfilm to be able to leave sets up, so they could come back and shoot newly written bits and pieces, if necessary." With a main building, nine independent soundstages, and one of the largest backlots in the world (one-hundred-plus acres), the site was also large enough to accommodate what promised to be a huge production.

an abandoned British aerodrome that had been used for years as an aircraft engine factory by Rolls Royce. The 286-acre site had subsequently been converted into a facility for film use.

Leavesden was perfect for the production of Episode I, for a number of reasons. Not only was there a tradition of shooting *Star Wars* movies in England—all three in the first trilogy had been shot at Elstree Studios—there was a practical consideration. McCallum was able to lease the facility for a full two and a half years, allowing the production company to leave sets up and return to pick up shots well after principal

Top left: Rick McCallum and George Lucas in the Episode I production offices at Leavesden Studios.
Top right, and left: The Naboo palace courtyard set under construction at Leavesden Studios.

Bocquet and his art department arrived at the studio first, followed in September by a crew of draftsmen. "Then," McCallum recalled, "in December, we started building the sets—very slowly. Traditionally, you throw a thousand people on a crew and they build the sets in a very short period of time—but you don't get to interact with them, and I didn't want George to have to go through that. So, instead, we'd have eight to twelve people building a set for a month. Throughout this entire period, we had a very small crew over in England—maybe twelve people."

In some respects, production design for Episode I was unconventional, since many of the designs for sets, locations, hardware, spacecraft, droids, and costumes had already been developed by Doug Chiang and his team in the two-year conceptualizing phase of preproduction. Bocquet's task was to design interiors, flesh out the already-developed designs, and make them, in McCallum's words, "a reality."

Bocquet began by familiarizing himself with the preliminary concepts and translating them into construction blueprints. Though some concessions to the physical world had to be made, Bocquet attempted to only improve the designs as they took shape in the real world, rather than compromise them. "We took the original drawings," Bocquet said, "and incorporated them into our designs, without betraying the initial concepts." For the Naboo spacecraft, for example, Chiang's team had conceived a sleek-looking exterior; but it was up to Bocquet and his team to design the interior. "We were completely responsible for the interior design of that ship, but we always stayed in line with the spirit of the way it looked on the outside."

Also in line with the original concepts were the real elements Bocquet incorporated into his designs, whenever possible. "All the *Star Wars* films have been based on real places, generally. So we tried to come up with environments and architectural styles that had some basis in reality, to give the audience something to key into. If you design things that are completely in the abstract, something not of this world, there is less chance that the audience will believe in it. George believes, rightly so, that the more real things you can get into your images, the more believable those images will be."

Another unusual aspect of Episode I's production design was that many of the film's environments and settings would be created through computer graphics—either in their entirety, or partially, with digital imagery being inserted into bluescreen areas surrounding the practical stage sets. Such a scheme required that Bocquet work in close collaboration with the CG team from Industrial Light & Magic. "We had to determine what portions of the sets should be constructed on the soundstages and what portions should be done on computer back at ILM," Bocquet explained. "Since we were producing part of the film long before the digital work was under way, we all had to make assumptions about what we should build and what could be better achieved at ILM."

While this "digital backlot" approach would be used more extensively in Episode I

In addition to full practical sets, Gavin Bocquet and his team also built partial sets surrounded by bluescreen to accommodate the later insertion of computer-generated set images.

than in any film in history, Bocquet was not a complete stranger to the technology, nor to the impact it would have on his production design assignment. "I didn't see the bluescreens or the effects as intrusions to my work," Bocquet related, "because those things have always been a part of what we do. Now it is CG that is allowing the director to extend sets and backgrounds; but the process is no different than it was years ago when they were extending sets through matte paintings or foreground miniatures. The idea is the same: here is an environment—how do we produce it in the most visually dynamic, yet economical way?"

Upon his arrival at Leavesden, Bocquet initiated the building of sets for the first

Above: Reggia Palace in Caserta, Italy, was chosen as the setting for the interiors of Queen Amidala's palace. Left: Director of photography David Tattersall and first assistant director Chris Newman.

part of the shooting schedule. A break in the middle of that schedule, during which the cast and crew would travel to locations in Italy and Tunisia, would give Bocquet and the construction crews time to strike those sets and erect new ones for the final weeks of filming. All together, Bocquet and his crew would build more than sixty sets—interiors on stage at Leavesden, and exteriors in Tunisia. "Even with all the digital sets we were going to be doing," McCallum noted, "we still had to build sixty to seventy sets. This movie was so plot-driven, every page and an eighth we were in a new set. There would be a minute's worth of dialogue and, boom, we'd be onto another set. It was constant plot, thrust, and movement. It was insane." To accomplish the sixty- to seventy-set build, a huge woodworking shop was eventually established at Leavesden, where up to one hundred carpenters labored for many months.

Most of the sets were first built in miniature, enabling Lucas to make minor adjustments and to plan camera moves and angles in advance. As is always the case in production, many of those preplanned camera angles were changed once Lucas was behind the camera; and so Bocquet attempted to make each set as flexible as possible, to accommodate last-minute changes in camera position and shot design.

Among the interior sets built at Leavesden for the first weeks of shooting were Palpatine's quarters, the Galactic Senate chamber, the Mos Espa arena pit hangar, Watto's junk shop, and Anakin's hovel—exteriors of which would be built in Tunisia. Anakin's home, in fact, was the first set built for the movie. "George wanted Anakin's hovel to look like Luke Skywalker's home in the first film," Bocquet said. "That set had featured sixties-style furniture and

an overall soft look, but with techie pieces here and there. Since we knew Anakin worked on things like the Podracer engines and his droid, we made his bedroom into a kind of workshop."

While no full sets would have to be built on location in Italy, rooms within the palace at Caserta—chosen as the setting for interiors of Queen Amidala's palace—did have to be dressed appropriately. Bocquet and Rick McCallum had discovered the palace when, early in preproduction, they had conducted their extensive location scout, driving roughly four thousand miles across Europe over the course of four weeks. Their travels included a week and a half in Portugal and another few weeks in Italy. "We were looking for grand palaces," Bocquet recalled, "grand corridors, grand rooms. It had to be monumental. At first, we weren't sure if we were going to find all the locations for the palace in one place." But, at the Reggia Palace in Caserta, they did find such a grand place. "As soon as we walked in, we felt we had found the right location."

McCallum and Bocquet feared, however, that Reggia Palace would not be available for filming, since it was an enormously popular tourist location. In fact, after the Vatican, the palace is one of the most visited sites in Italy. Fortunately, McCallum's production team was able to negotiate a schedule with the director of the palace that would allow the production to shoot there for four days. "It was tricky at first," McCallum admitted, "but we were able to work out a schedule in which we'd start shooting after the palace was closed to the public, from about midday to midnight." Certain palace interiors would still have to be built at Leavesden to accommodate scenes that featured explosions orchestrated by special effects coordinator Peter Hutchinson and his crew.

The next location stop on the schedule would be Tunisia, where all the Tatooine exteriors would be filmed—just as they were for the original *Star Wars*. For the sake of continuity, Lucas had hoped to return to the same Tunisian locations. "George loves the light, the color of the sand, and the atmosphere in Tunisia," Bocquet commented.

Surprisingly, because only loose records had been kept, no one was entirely sure, at the start, just *where* those original sites were located. But then a fortuitous letter was sent to Lucasfilm. "It was from an archaeologist, David West Reynolds," McCallum said, "who had traveled to Tunesia to research the original sites of *Star Wars*. He knew exactly where the locations were! So we brought him on, and he later wound up working here at Skywalker Ranch."

When the original Tunisian locations

Scenes on the desert planet of Tatooine were filmed in Tunisia, just as they had been for the first *Star Wars*. Since the original Tunisian sites had grown too modernized, production had to find locations in other regions of the country.

Prop department head Ty Teiger and set decorator Peter Walpole devised hundreds of *Star Wars*–style props for the film.
Above: The kitchen in the Skywalker hovel.
Right: Lightsabers.

were scouted, however, McCallum and Bocquet found that they were unsuitably modernized now, twenty years after the making of *Star Wars*. Tatooine-like locations were discovered nearby, however, in Tozeur, Medenine, and Hadada. Finding the Tunisian locations was particularly satisfying for Rick McCallum. "We could immediately visualize the town and all the buildings," McCallum said. "I felt as if Mos Espa was coming alive in front of my very eyes."

Working closely with Bocquet throughout the build were prop department head Ty Teiger and set decorator Peter Walpole, who built an array of *Star Wars*–style props, both from scratch and by mixing and matching existing pieces. Qui-Gon's communication device, the comlink, for example, was assembled with parts from a lady's electric razor. Hundreds of gadgets were built, as were prop guns, fashioned out of wood and resin, then painted to give them a metallic sheen.

The lightsabers were modified only slightly from the ones already familiar to *Star Wars* fans—although they would see much more use in Episode I. "I wanted to use the lightsaber a lot more in this film," Lucas noted. "It is a wonderful weapon, because

you can do almost anything with it. It is the ultimate weapon, even though it is not very high-tech. For this movie, I wanted something that was lethal, but elegant and sophisticated." A new lightsaber design would be the double-sided saber used by Darth Maul in his duel with Qui-Gon and Obi-Wan. As in the original films, the visual effects team later would add the actual glowing saber effect.

One of the biggest prop assignments was the building of the Podracers, which would ultimately combine elements of the concept art illustrations with Bocquet's and the prop department's designs. To gather basic building materials for the Podracers, Rick McCallum, Peter Walpole, and Gavin Bocquet went to Arizona, where they purchased $60,000 worth of surplus military aircraft parts. "We wound up with eighteen cockpits and engines—half of which were inspired by

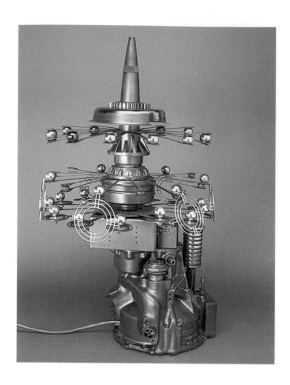

Doug Chiang's team and half that were conceived by ours," Bocquet explained. "Because of this mix, there was a richness to the Podracers that you wouldn't find had all of them come out of the same mind."

A closely related department was wardrobe, headed by costume designer Trisha Biggar, another veteran of *The Young Indiana Jones Chronicles*. Art director Iain McCaig had designed the costumes as sketches dur-

ing the two-year concept art phase, but it was Biggar's job to translate those drawings into functional costumes. "It is one thing to design and sketch a costume on paper," George Lucas noted, "and quite another to actually build it. Trisha and I would sit and look at the designs, trying to figure out how they would work in reality. She'd point to something on the drawing and ask, 'What's this?' And I'd say, 'It's a pencil flare.' Well, a pencil flare looked great in a drawing, but it couldn't be translated into the real thing. Trisha had a huge job in just translating all of these designs into cloth and fabric and

Above: Some of the props and weapons were built from scratch, others were assembled from bits and pieces of existing electronic and mechanical items.
Left: Costume designer Trisha Biggar.

60

materials that would actually work and not look silly."

Biggar's assignment was also an organizational and logistical challenge, since the show would require the building, from scratch, of over eleven hundred complete costumes. "Just making that many costumes," Lucas said, "getting them manufactured and getting them to the set on time was a huge job. Trisha also had to work out all the colors of the costumes, and how those colors would play against the colors on the sets. We had endless discussions about various shades of colors and what I wanted, color-wise, on each set. She would take fabrics and stand them on the sets, or do mockups of various costumes to see if they would work in those sets. There were a lot of complex things that had to be dealt with."

Accessories also fell under Biggar's

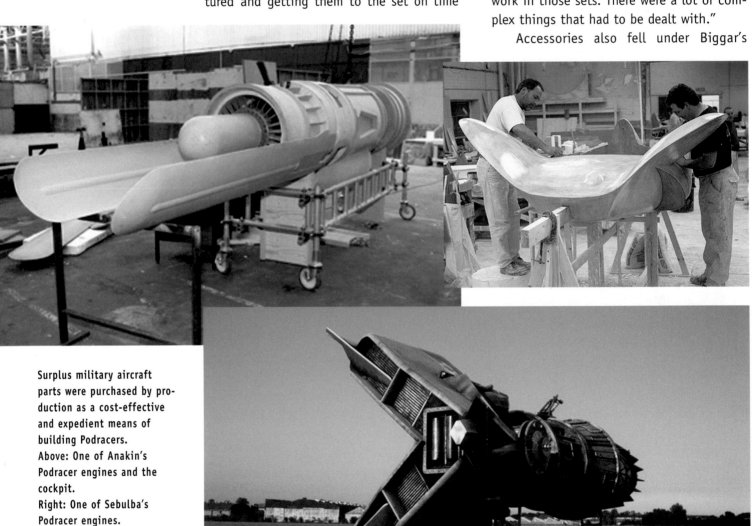

Surplus military aircraft parts were purchased by production as a cost-effective and expedient means of building Podracers.
Above: One of Anakin's Podracer engines and the cockpit.
Right: One of Sebulba's Podracer engines.

Far left: Queen Amidala in military garb.
Left: The costume worn by Alec Guinness in the original *Star Wars* was meticulously redesigned for Ewan McGregor.

domain. "Whether it was a beaded necklace or a holster for a pistol or a helmet, that was her responsibility. The list went on and on. And not only did all of that stuff have to be built, it had to be maintained throughout the making of the movie. Trisha did a fantastic job of managing this huge undertaking."

Biggar initiated that undertaking by first studying Iain McCaig's drawings and making herself familiar with the various cultural influences at work. "There was an Asian influence," Biggar said, "but there was also a mixture of North African and fourteenth- and fifteenth-century Europe." Once costume concepts were approved, Biggar set up a huge wardrobe department at Leavesden Studios that included a costume prop depart-

ment—where headdresses and armor were made—a dye room, and an accessory department responsible for making hats, jewelry, and other wardrobe accoutrements. Two hundred fifty costumes were built for principals, while background characters—human and otherwise—required an additional five thousand pieces of clothing, all of which were created from scratch.

But Biggar had to concern herself with more than sheer volume and the style of costume; she also had to consult with stunt coordinator Nick Gillard, as well as the art and creature departments, to ensure the costumes would accommodate the action sequences. "We had to work very closely with the creature and stunt departments," Biggar

A variety of extraordinary, ornate gowns was designed for the character of Queen Amidala.

said. "By consulting with them, we learned which fabrics we could use, and which would restrict characters' movement. We also had to stick to fabrics that wouldn't wear too heavily on the material used to make the creatures' skins."

An additional task in building the costumes for Obi-Wan was matching the look established in the costumes worn by Alec Guinness in the original *Star Wars*. "We had the original costume sent to us from the archives at Skywalker Ranch," Biggar explained. "The costume was twenty years old, so we had to do quite a bit of testing to see how we could 'freshen up' the look. We presented George with a variety of shades until he was satisfied."

The most challenging character to dress, however—and the most rewarding—was young Queen Amidala, who would be seen in a variety of extraordinary gowns in the course of the story. The overall style for the Queen's wardrobe was reminiscent of the Italian Renaissance period, and the color palette was meant to suggest those shades found in Italian architecture. "The costumes for the Queen were all very large," Biggar noted. "Each had a very different look, and there was a different style of costume for each part of the film. They were also very heavy, made from a variety of fabrics."

The showstopper of the Queen's gowns is the one she wears for the ceremonial parade in the film's finale. Lucas had envisioned a dress that would convey a sense of joy and celebration. "It had to be very light and beautiful," Biggar said, "with the feeling of a wedding dress. George also liked a drawing Iain McCaig had done that showed a very large, unusual collar at the back of the dress." With McCaig, Biggar sorted through many possible fabrics and colors for the dress and built several versions until a final design was approved.

Just as the costumes and many of the

film's environments had been predesigned by the art department, most of the alien characters that would populate the film had been developed by the time crews arrived at Leavesden to begin building the production. But it was up to creature effects supervisor Nick Dudman to create many of those characters, either as animatronic puppets or as masks and suits that would be worn by performers.

Appropriately, Dudman got his start in films as an apprentice to British makeup artist Stuart Freeborn, working on the character of Yoda for *The Empire Strikes Back*. Since then, Dudman had worked on several Lucasfilm productions, including *Return of the Jedi, Willow*, and *Indiana Jones and the Last Crusade*. Dudman was already at Leavesden, working on *Mortal Kombat: Annihilation* when he received a visit from Rick McCallum. Two days later, he was on board Episode I.

"Nick had a very tough job in front of him," McCallum conceded, "because he had a lot of creatures to design and build in only six months. I'd actually hired him a year ear-

lier, but we couldn't let him get started until January 1997—just six months before the shoot—because we were still waiting to see how far we were going to push CG. We wanted to do as many characters through CG as possible. For a long time we didn't know for sure which characters or how many would have to be done with puppets or masks. Eventually, it came down to cost. There were some characters that would be cheaper and easier to do with animatronic puppets and masks—and those were the characters that fell into Nick's lap just a few months before production."

Dudman started the assignment by visiting Skywalker Ranch, where he explored the Ranch archives to determine which of the original creatures might be reused for the new film. While there, he also read the script and did a breakdown of all the scenes that would involve practical creatures. "I would look at a character and ask myself, 'Can we fit a person in there?'" Dudman explained. "If the answer was yes, then it would be done with a suit, or possibly just a prosthetic makeup, if the effect was subtle enough. If it was a character that couldn't accommodate a performer inside, then it had to be a puppet." Some creatures were so outlandish, they could only be done as computer-generated characters. "The creatures involved in the Podrace, for example, are primarily CG. But for the street scenes on Tatooine, we created every possible alien we could come up with."

When he returned to Leavesden, Dudman assembled a team that included Chris Barton, who would handle all the animatronics and engineering chores, key sculptor Gary Pollard, and bodysuit fabricator Monique Brown. In total, a team of fifty-five craftspeople was required to create the movie's many creatures.

Among the first to be featured in the film were the Neimoidians, Nute and Rune, who orchestrate—with the Sith Lords—the invasion of Naboo. The Neimoidians were added to Dudman's slate rather late in the creature build, however, since they had been designated as CG characters until just twelve weeks before the start of principal photography. "Again," McCallum explained, "it was just a matter of economics. For as little screen time as these characters would have, it was faster and cheaper to do them with actors in masks and suits."

Once the decision had been made to do the Neimoidians practically, actors Silas Carson and Jerome Blake were cast in the roles of Nute and Rune. With little time to build the characters, Dudman and his team created animatronic puppet heads that were capable of lip sync, delivering them just one day before they were due to appear on the set. The heads would be worn by Carson and Blake, but were themselves radio controlled. "My key sculptor, Gary Pollard, has an amaz-

ing ability to create an entire race of characters out of the most simple forms," Dudman commented. "He was able to sculpt Neimoidians that not only looked interesting, but also looked different from one another."

The senators featured in the Senate chamber sequence and the background Jedi Council members were also key characters

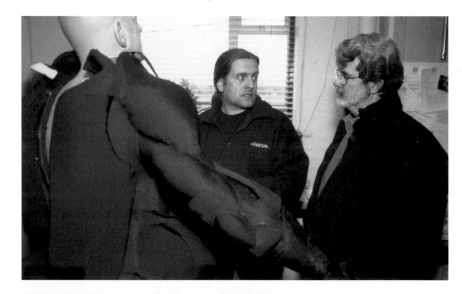

Lucas toured all of the production departments on a daily basis.
Above: Lucas checks on the progress of creature designs with Nick Dudman, creature design effects supervisor.
Left: Lucas inspects a mask for the alien Gamorrean species.

built by Dudman. Several designs had been developed by the art department at Skywalker Ranch, designated simply with numbers: Senator 1, Senator 2, Jedi 1, Jedi 2, and so on. "We had to come up with names for them," Dudman said. "I decided to call one of the Jedi Plonkoon, because we called my son that during the first year of his life. I wrote down Plonkoon, George crossed out the *n* and Plo Koon was born! Swokes came from my wife's name, Sue Oaks, and George went with that."

Although Jar Jar Binks was always going to be a CG character, Dudman's team was tasked with building a suit and headpiece that would be worn by Jar Jar performer Ahmed Best. The head, worn on top of Best's own, would make the actor the same six-foot-plus height of the character—thus ensuring the eyelines would be correct when other actors interacted with Jar Jar. The multicolored suit would provide ILM with vital lighting reference from the set. Built from a

Top: For the Neimoidians, animatronic heads capable of lip-sync action were created. Here, key sculptor Gary Pollard works on the head for the viceroy Rune Haako.

Middle: Actor Jerome Blake poses with his character's radio-controlled head prior to shooting.

Bottom: The actors inside the heads, Jerome Blake and Silas Carson, were cooled between takes by air pumped through a tube.

lifecast of Best, the suit was extraordinarily well fitted. "We were very pleased," Dudman commented. "It didn't even look like he was wearing a suit, it fit him so well. It just looked like body painting."

In addition to new characters, Dudman and his team reprised creatures from the original trilogy—most notably, the Jedi Master Yoda. This would be a younger Yoda, however, as well as a new and improved version. While the original Yoda—designed by Stuart Freeborn—had been made out of foam latex, the Episode I character was fashioned out of silicone, a much more realistic,

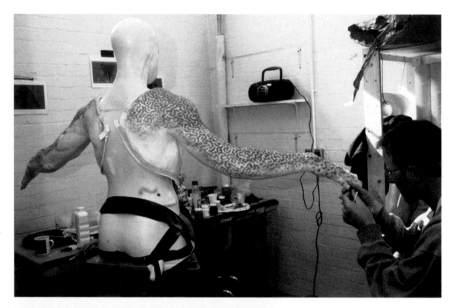

Above, left and right: The on-set Jar Jar suit under construction.
Left: Practical masks, suits, and prosthetic makeup were required for sequences such as those in the senate chamber and the Jedi Council.

fleshier material that would give the puppet greater freedom of movement. Improvements were also made in the puppet's mechanisms—particularly after discussions with Frank Oz, who had originally puppeteered the character and provided the voice, as he would do again for Episode I.

Oz recalled that one of the difficulties in puppeteering the original Yoda was that he had to carry the puppet's weight on his middle finger, also used to operate the character's eyebrows. In addition, because of the configuration of the mechanisms, each time Yoda's brows moved, his mouth would move as well. For the new Yoda, the brow control was taken away from the main puppeteer and radio-controlled by another operator from off camera. A smile mechanism was also added—although the actual lip-syncing would still be performed by Oz, to match what had been done in the previous films.

Wookiees would also make a repeat appearance, specifically in the Senate sequence in Coruscant. Rather than make a new Wookiee suit, Dudman pulled the old Chewbacca costume out of the Lucasfilm archives. To create the illusion of three Wookiees, the suit—fitted on a performer—was shot separately, three different times, altered slightly for each individual shot. "We would move the Wookiee into a new position on the set and add more or less white hair to it," Dudman revealed. "When the shots were put together, we ended up with three different Wookiees out of one suit."

Dudman and his crew would work for several months on the Episode I project, which became a huge challenge as more creatures were added to their slate. "The

scale of the movie was colossal," Dudman offered. "We created over a hundred forty separate aliens in a short period of time. And we couldn't escape the fact that our work was going to be judged against the work that was done before. There is a very critical audience out there that knows the minutiae of the world George Lucas has created. We knew if we made mistakes, they would pick up on them. Living up to the expectations of the fans was a lot of pressure."

Above left: ILM visual effects supervisor John Knoll was a constant on-set presence during the shoot. Here, Knoll with producer Rick McCallum.
Above right: Mike Lynch, from ILM's model shop, demonstrates the Japanese puppeteering technique used to articulate C-3PO on the set.

Among those expectations was that the droids R2-D2 and C-3PO would be featured in the new movie—and Lucas did not disappoint. A Leavesden crew under radio-control specialist and chief operator Jolyon Bambridge built over a dozen new R2-D2 units for use in Episode I, in addition to two units that were refitted from the classic trilogy. In addition to the new R2-D2s assembled in England, a crew at ILM developed an upgraded model of its own, powered by wheelchair motors. This unit and its operator, Don Bies, were flown to England and added to the pool of specialized performing robots that could now handle virtually any kind of terrain. Finally, to give R2-D2 a human dimension in certain shots, actor Kenny Baker was hidden inside one of the suits, just as he had been for all three original *Star Wars* movies.

C-3PO's design would be modified even more to resemble a skeletal understructure of the droid as he appeared in the first three films. Since the design precluded putting an actor in a suit, the effects crew at ILM took on the assignment of realizing C-3PO. "We knew it would either have to be computer generated or a puppet of some kind," visual effects supervisor John Knoll explained. Both Knoll and Lucas were familiar with a Japanese puppeteering technique in which the puppeteer dresses in black and stands in front of a black background as he manipulates a puppet in front of his body—and both thought the technique might work for C-3PO. Mike Lynch from ILM's model shop made a crude mock-up puppet, operated by a puppeteer dressed in black, and photographed by John Knoll. The results of the test were promising. "From those tests, we decided that we could shoot scenes with Threepio on the set, and remove the performer digitally later on." With the advent of digital technology, removal of puppeteers and operators has become a standard technique in filmmaking. Bits and pieces of imagery are digitally extracted from a "clean plate"—a plate that does not feature the puppeteer or the puppet—and are patched

C-3PO's operator—who stood directly behind the puppet—was dressed in an easily isolated color to ease the digital removal of the puppeteer in postproduction.

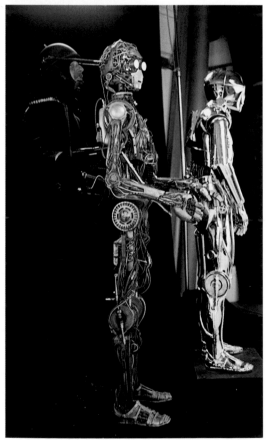

into the offending areas, thereby "removing" rigs, wires, or, as in this case, entire human beings.

Once on the set, Mike Lynch operated the C-3PO puppet as actor Anthony Daniels spoke C-3PO's lines from off camera. "Mike had to react to what Anthony was saying," Knoll said, "and move the puppet accordingly."

In addition to the two "star" droids, ILM's model shop provided full-scale versions of the battle and destroyer droids, which were used on set for lighting reference and to establish eyelines. All the battle and destroyer droids featured in the film would be computer generated. "We built ten droids," McCallum said, "but they were for placement only, so they weren't articulated at all. In other cases, we'd have extras dressed in white stand in for the droids on the set, just to give the actors a sense of where they would be in the scene."

While the building of sets, costumes, props, creatures, and droids would continue throughout production, those elements required for the beginning of the shoot were in place by the time George Lucas arrived at Leavesden in June 1997. After three years of preparation, it was time, at last, for cameras to roll on *Star Wars:* Episode I *The Phantom Menace.*

"I guess I'm back."

On Thursday, June 26, 1997, JAK Productions—the company formed specifically for the making of Episode I, and named for the first initials of George Lucas's three children—began principal photography. It was a momentous day, in many respects: a day that had been planned for and worked toward for more than two years; the first day of shooting on a new *Star Wars* episode in fifteen years; and the first time George Lucas had directed a movie in twenty years.

And yet, as is so often the case with momentous occasions, to the people most intimately involved, it felt like just another day. "Before you start shooting," Lucas

observed, "you're in preproduction for months. You go to the studio every day and you look at things and you answer thousands of questions. And when you start filming, you have actors and a camera, but basically you continue to answer thousands of questions—so it feels like a regular day. Sometimes you even forget you're filming a movie. But as soon as Liam Neeson walked on the set, dressed as a Jedi, I said to myself, 'I guess I'm back.' It was as if those twenty years had never elapsed."

Lucas had always intended to direct Episode I. On both *The Empire Strikes Back* and *Return of the Jedi*, he had spent as much time on the set as the film directors—so there seemed, in his mind, little reason to turn the reins of Episode I over to someone else. "As much as I *wanted* to hand over the last two films to other directors," Lucas noted, "I ended up being there all the time, and I had to work as hard as if I was directing anyway. The other reason I wanted to direct Episode I was that we were going to be attempting new things; and, in truth, I didn't quite know how we were going to do them—nobody did. So I figured I needed to be there at all times."

In the media, much would be made of Lucas's return to directing after a twenty-year absence; and yet, for Lucas himself, the transition from producing to directing was of

little consequence. "I've been very involved in my films all along," Lucas said. "I just haven't been down on the floor, actually doing the directing. In some ways, it is almost easier to direct it yourself, rather than have to tell somebody else to do this or that. But it was not all that different; and it wasn't a hard thing to get reacquainted with. It was almost as if I'd never stopped directing. In the end, all it meant was that I had to get up early in the morning and go to the set, whether I wanted to or not. And I couldn't do anything else for those three months—which was kind of fun and liberating. The company had to run itself, and all of my other problems had to go out the window.

"The parts of making a movie that I like best are the writing and editing, and I've been doing those all along. It's like building a house. I've been involved in doing up the plans and blueprints, and I've been in on the process of actually constructing the house. The part I haven't done is actually go out and collect the material. I haven't cut down the trees and milled the wood and put it on a truck. That's the way I see my involvement in the filmmaking process for the past twenty years—I've skipped the part where you collect the material, because it's not as much fun."

Lucas would be "collecting the material" for Episode I, however; and working alongside him throughout was Rick McCallum. On a typical day, McCallum would get to the studio about two hours before Lucas to confer

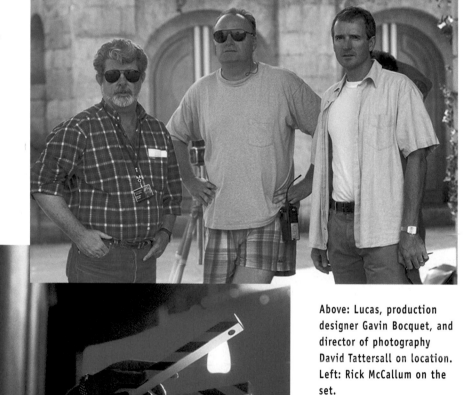

Above: Lucas, production designer Gavin Bocquet, and director of photography David Tattersall on location. Left: Rick McCallum on the set.

with department heads regarding the day's work. "On a film like this," McCallum said, "the last thing we needed was departments working against each other—yet that is something I've seen happen on many movies." At the end of the day, McCallum would meet again with department heads and Lucas to discuss the following day's schedule, the next set, or the next location, ensuring everything was on track.

Another key collaborator with Lucas during the three-month shoot was director of photography David Tattersall. Tattersall's credits included *Con Air, Moll Flanders*, and *The Green Mile*; and, like so many of the principal crew members, he had worked on *The Young Indiana Jones Chronicles*, shooting about thirty of the television episodes. "David Tattersall and others we hired from *Young Indy* knew the kinds of tricks we would be using on this movie," Lucas explained. "We'd evolved a lot of new ways of doing production over the course of the TV series, and we were going to be doing the same things for Episode I. There was a language that had been developed in the course of doing that series, and a way of doing things,

During production, Lucas maintained a constant on-set dialogue with Tattersall, who was hired just five weeks before the start of principal photography.

that had taken us four or five years to get down. I wanted to continue it on this film, without having to train a whole new group of people. There was a way the crew would have to light things that weren't actually there, for example, which David understood from his experience on the TV show."

Hired just five weeks before the start of principal photography, Tattersall launched the assignment by looking at the art department's paintings, drawings, storyboards, and animatics to absorb the look and style of the movie Lucas envisioned. More inspiration was sought by watching many classic science fiction and fantasy films. But Tattersall soon realized that the best way to prepare himself for the filming of Episode I was to view, and review, the original trilogy. *A New Hope* was particularly illuminating, since Episode I would return to some of the sites and locations featured in that first film. The animatics prepared by the art department were also a good reference for developing a sense of timing and camera movement for each of the action scenes.

Once on the set, Tattersall often referred to the film's "bible"—a huge binder filled with storyboards of the movie's original five thousand shots. These storyboards were color coded to designate which shots would be computer generated (CG), which would be live-action, and which would be filmed in front of a bluescreen.

"A full 65 to 75 percent of our scenes were going to be shot with at least some bluescreen," Rick McCallum noted. "We only built as much of the sets as we absolutely had to—and the rest would be done through CG, with those elements matted into the bluescreen areas. Because we had the animatics for all the sequences, and because George was willing to commit to those animatics once he was on the set, we knew how much of the sets had to be built. We would only build up to the heights of the actors, for example. Liam was so tall, he cost us another $150,000 in set construction because we had to build all the way up to his full height in any of the sets he'd be in."

The set-building approach was yet another means to minimize costs and streamline the filmmaking process. "There is horrendous waste in most movies," McCallum explained. "Art directors will overbuild sets, just in case the director changes his mind about how a shot is going to move or be framed. The script will say that a guy walks through a kitchen—and they'll build a whole kitchen, even though it will never be seen! We didn't do any of that. We built as little as we could get away with, and then put up bluescreens, just in case it needed to be filled out a bit more. We'd take stills of every single position on the set, and we could use those stills as patches to fill in if we needed them later. If we needed another six feet of set, we'd just slap up a bluescreen and composite that still into the blue area later."

Bluescreen photography—which, typi-cally, requires meticulous lighting to avoid blue spill reflections on the sets and actors and to ensure clean, usable matte areas— was of particular concern to Tattersall and the entire lighting and camera crew. "We knew that bluescreens would be a part of most of the sequences," Tattersall remarked, "so I had to come up with a quick and reli-able way to light them." Since many of the screens would be quite tall—up to twenty feet—and/or quite long (such as the three-hundred-foot bluescreen used to surround

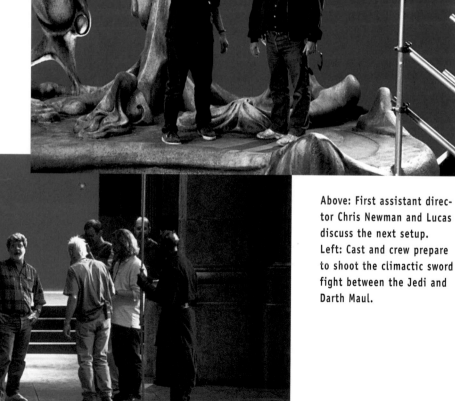

Above: First assistant direc-tor Chris Newman and Lucas discuss the next setup.
Left: Cast and crew prepare to shoot the climactic sword fight between the Jedi and Darth Maul.

Despite the large number of potentially time-consuming bluescreen shots, John Knoll and David Tattersall were able to keep up an astounding pace of thirty-six setups per day.

Palpatine's headquarters, the Jedi Council chamber, and the hangar at Theed) the lighting had to evenly illuminate a large expanse. "We tested different types of lamps, as well as different types of bluescreens. A company in England came up with a new type of lamp that was twice as powerful as what was available on the market. We could set up two banks of those lamps, one up high and one near the ground, approximately sixty feet from the screen, and we would get this beautiful flat coverage." Blue spill on shiny floors or marble surfaces was suppressed in the footage through a special software program written by John Knoll.

Knoll, too, had concerns about the amount of bluescreen work that the show would require—especially considering the pace at which the crew would have to work. Only sixty-five days had been allotted for the entire principal photography schedule. With so few shooting days, Lucas and his crew had to do thirty-six camera setups a day. "We didn't leave until we'd done thirty-six setups," McCallum stated. "If that was five o'clock, we left at five o'clock. But if it wasn't until ten o'clock, we didn't leave until ten o'clock." At thirty-six setups per day, and a majority of them involving bluescreen, the

crew would not have the time to meticulously light each and every bluescreen shot. "John was a bit nervous about that at first. But I put it to him, 'Do you want everybody to come to work at seven o'clock in the morning and not leave until midnight every night? Because that's what you're asking me to do to everybody if we have to take this much time with the bluescreen.' I didn't want to do that, and neither did he. And by the second week, he saw there was no reason for it anyway. John realized that no matter what problem arose with the bluescreen elements, there'd be some way to fix it down the line. Moving quickly from setup to setup was more important."

Just as *The Young Indiana Jones Chronicles* had been a testing ground for Episode I, Episode I would be a testing ground for the two subsequent *Star Wars* chapters. Among the innovations Lucas and McCallum wanted to test on this first film of the trilogy was shooting with high-definition digital tape, as opposed to film. Since the entire movie would be digitized from film for the compositing of CG effects anyway—as will the next two films—the more economical approach was to shoot on digital videotape to begin with, then record that back out to film for distribution, once the movie was entirely assembled. The plan had merit—as long as the digital video imagery could hold up, in terms of quality, when compared against film.

As a test, Lucas and McCallum had a handful of shots done on the high-definition digital tape, then inserted those shots back-to-back with filmed images. "George wanted to shoot ten or twenty shots that would be in the movie on high-def," McCallum explained, "just to see how well they would integrate with the filmed stuff. We did some high-def shots of crowds in the backgrounds

Left: The set of Palpatine's quarters.
Below: Captured on the first day of shooting was a scene between Darth Maul and Darth Sidious on a balcony overlooking Coruscant. A balcony set piece was backed by bluescreen, and a digitally rendered view of Coruscant was composited into the blue area in post-production.

of the Podrace, and other shots throughout the movie—one shot of Anakin, for example, and one of Qui-Gon. We wanted to see if we could get one shot in high-def, then cut away, and then cut back to film, without it being noticeable. And we discovered we could. It worked beautifully. In fact, Episode I is probably the last movie we'll be shooting on film. From here on out, we're no longer going to shoot with film—it will be a totally digital thing. No film cameras will be involved at all."

The first month of shooting was situated at Leavesden Studios, and the first scene on the shooting schedule for June 26, 1997, was one between Darth Maul and Darth Sidious on a balcony on Coruscant, overlooking the capital city. For now, the balcony set only overlooked a bluescreen area, as the city would be computer generated by ILM in postproduction. The set was buzzing with activity, and security was tight. Everyone

was required to wear a name tag—even George Lucas, whose tag read "Yoda."

Also scheduled for that first day was a scene in Palpatine's quarters between Ian McDiarmid as Palpatine and Natalie Portman as Queen Amidala. "Walking on the set that first day was literally like going back in time to my experience on *Return of the Jedi*,"

McDiarmid said. "George said, 'Action,' and I was that character once again—though a younger version of that character. There was definitely a high degree of electricity. It was, after all, a historic moment."

Orchestrating that day's shoot—and all the days to follow—was first assistant director Chris Newman. Newman would act as the direct link between Lucas and the crew, going over the schedule with the former and ensuring that everything ran as smoothly as possible with the latter. "It was like playing chess," Newman said, "and the stakes were quite high. Part of the pressure was that nobody had worked with George as a director for a long time, so nobody knew what he would be like, or what to expect. I was also nervous because I was working with a new crew. Rick McCallum had put a lot of faith in me by hiring me, and I wanted to make sure that faith was justified. We were all testing the waters."

Gavin Bocquet and crew had realized a

set for Palpatine's quarters that was rich in burgundies and scarlet reds. The Emperor's guards in *Return of the Jedi* had inspired the color scheme for the set. "We wanted Palpatine's quarters to have a very strong personality," Bocquet said, "and to be unique to his character. The best way to convey those things was through color. We finished the set completely just one day before shooting began. Fortunately, George loved it."

For his role as Darth Maul, Ray Park arrived on set in full makeup and costume. Makeup artist Paul Engelen, who did his early training with *Star Wars* alum Stuart Freeborn, supervised the transformation, which consisted of a tattoo covering Park's face. "For the tattoo," Engelen explained, "we used an alcohol-based pigment and applied it like paint."

Nick Dudman's shop had produced several sets of horns that would protrude out of Darth Maul's skull. "I originally had the horns growing *through* the skull," Dudman said, "but George liked a raised area around

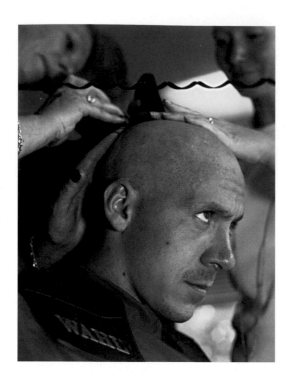

them better. I thought of them as weapons; and they do actually look like shark's teeth. To avoid injuries, we used rubber horns on him for the most serious stunts and action scenes." To make Darth Maul's teeth look rotten and decaying, an acrylic coloring was applied, while special contact lenses gave the character his reptilian eyes.

Due to the efficiency of the cast and crew, the requisite thirty-plus setups were accomplished that first day of filming. "We were able to keep that average for the next sixty-five days," David Tattersall said. "It was a really good way to make the film. I think the fact that we worked so fast gave the scenes more spontaneity and an unusual edge."

Among the key scenes filmed in the next few days at Leavesden was the Galactic Senate sequence. Since much of the Senate chamber set—including the flying platforms—would be built digitally in postproduction, the scene was particularly difficult from a technical standpoint, requiring that

the actors work in front of bluescreens and use their imaginations to determine where digital set pieces and characters would eventually be positioned. "The Senate chamber was very difficult in terms of figuring out where everybody was and whether the actors should be looking up or down as all these flying boxes floated in and out," Lucas said. "I tried to make things easier for everyone when I could. For example, we had people standing in for some of the CG characters, so the actors would have someone to relate to. I would do most of the effects scenes with the actors playing against the CG stand-ins first. Then we would shoot the scene again without the stand-ins, to give us a clean plate that ILM could work with later."

Park spent hours in makeup for the transformation into the Sith lord.

Episode I would push the envelope in its use of bluescreen and computer generated set extensions. Below left: A scene in the galactic senate chamber. Set pieces were shot in front of blue, with the majority of the chamber created in the digital realm.
Below right: Liam Neeson and George Lucas on the set.
Bottom: The senate chamber box for the Ithorian delegation.

Stand-ins working in a partial set, surrounded mainly by blue, was a difficult acting situation to adjust to—especially since none of the principal actors had *ever* performed in front of a bluescreen prior to Episode I. "Ewan didn't even know what a bluescreen was," McCallum said. "But we did as much as we could to ground them in the scenes. Not only did we have stand-ins for the CG characters, we also had the animatics to show the actors, so they could see, in rough form, how the scene would play out once everything was together. We also had a lot of rehearsal time for them, and we gave all the

actors a folder of the artwork, so they understood how things were going to look. It took about ten days or two weeks before everyone felt really comfortable with the bluescreen."

"The whole technical aspect of the film could have been terribly intimidating," Liam Neeson conceded, "but the fact that George has mastered that technology, and in fact

had a hand in developing much of it, was very comforting for the cast. It created an absolute ease on the set."

Also instrumental in easing the technical aspects of the shoot were visual effects supervisor John Knoll and a small crew from Industrial Light & Magic. Knoll's credentials were impressive. A thirteen-year veteran of Industrial Light & Magic, he had codeveloped Photoshop, one of the most widely used computer graphics packages on the market, and had served as visual effects supervisor on Brian De Palma's *Mission: Impossible* and the *Star Wars Special Editions*, as well as numerous commercials.

Knoll had prepared for his supervisory role very early on, reading the script and studying more than three thousand storyboards. "George and I would go through the boards," Knoll recalled, "and mark which shots would be live-action, which would be

CG, which would be a miniature or a matte painting—et cetera. Then, over the months that followed, before shooting started, I had a chance to evaluate how we were going to execute the effects."

Knoll would be on the set nearly every day of production. "He was gone for nine days in the middle of the schedule when he went back to ILM to check on the development of the Podrace," McCallum recalled. "But other than that, he was there every day. In addition to John, we had Jack Haye from ILM, who did all the laser measurements of the sets for match-moving purposes. And then, to help him, we hired local kids that Jack trained." The measuring of the sets with laser-surveying equipment was standard procedure for shots that would eventually include digital imagery. Such measurements, along with information about the camera lens and other particulars, would enable the match-movers at ILM to sync their virtual camera up with the live-action one, replicating its movements exactly.

Knoll's most pressing duty on the set was to ensure the plates being captured during live-action photography would be suitable for the postproduction visual effects

Above left to right: Jack Haye, digital camera matchmover; Bernard Hearn, dressing propman; and Craig Narramore, assistant, take measurements on the set of the Theed main hangar at Leavesden Studios.
Left: Reference footage of source lights hitting a sphere was filmed before or after each shot so that on-set lighting could be later replicated on the CG images.

effort. "While we were shooting," Lucas recalled, "I usually had the effects people from ILM on the set right next to me. So when I composed a shot, I could turn to them, and say, 'Can you guys live with this?' I wanted to make sure that I wasn't doing anything that would jeopardize the shots from their end later on."

It was also Knoll's responsibility to shoot reference material on the set—material that would prove critical when it came time to produce the visual effects shots. "It's extremely important, when you're creating a CG character in a shot, to get the lighting right," Knoll said. "The best way to do that is to capture the lighting that was on the set at the same point where the CG character will eventually be inserted." Partial full-size models or half-size models of main CG characters, such as Jar Jar, Watto, and Sebulba, were provided to the production crew. By shooting a reference plate with these fully painted props on the set, ILM would have an excellent guide for re-creating shadows and lighting when the CG versions of the characters were inserted into the scenes.

To ensure a smooth, working collaboration between the live-action and visual

effects crews, Knoll maintained a constant dialogue with David Tattersall, whose lighting of sets would greatly impact the visual effects elements added when production had wrapped. Relatively new technology was also useful in making sure that on-set camera moves could be duplicated when shooting those elements. Cameras were rigged with data-capture modules that recorded the moves to a laptop computer. "Arri Media, our camera supplier for years, built this data-capture system to ILM's design specifications," McCallum explained. "It would record the lens, the focal length, the focus, and also the tilt and pan of the camera. We wanted to be able to download that information immediately into a computer, where a CG artist could later use it to find the 3-D dimensions within the frame."

Match-moving, the process by which the live-action camera moves are painstakingly matched in the virtual realm, would still be

Full- or half-size models of key CG characters were also used on the set as a means of gathering vital lighting and shadow reference.

a requirement, however, despite the computer assist on set. "It was a new system, and we weren't sure how well it would work. So match-moving was still necessary, just in case the data was corrupted. But the system worked brilliantly; and it will be used even more for the next two movies. The old way, we had to scan in a piece of film, and then a match-mover would have to sit in front of the monitor and try to figure out distances, angles, everything. It could take a week just to figure all of that stuff out for the virtual camera. With this new system, all of that information will be programmed in, and the CG operator will be able to automatically play back the camera move in the virtual environment."

July 2, 1997, was the first day of shooting for many of the principal actors. Among those present were Liam Neeson, Ewan McGregor, Natalie Portman, Jake Lloyd, Kenny Baker, Terence Stamp, and Ahmed

Prod. Office: Leavesden Studios		JAK PRODUCTIONS LTD STAR WARS - EPISODE 1 THE BEGINNING		Date: Wednesday 2 July 1997 Call Sheet No: 5		
				UNIT CALL ON SET: 8.00am B/fast in canteen from 7.00am		
Director: George Lucas Producer: Rick McCallum						
		NO SMOKING ON SET				
LOCATION	SET - DESCRIPTION		SCENE	D/N	PGs	CAST
FS1a STAGE Leavesden Studio	Ext Coruscant-Senate Landing Platform Valorum & Palpatine meet group off Naboo craft		126pt	D	1 3/8	1.2.3.5.6.9.10.11.14. 44.47.68.
	Ext Coruscant-Senate Landing Platform Taxi en route		126pt	D	1/8	2.3.6.9.10.11.47.68.
(See map attached)						

	ARTISTE	CHARACTER	DR	P.UP	M.UP/W L.UP	ON SET
1	Liam Neeson	Qui-Gon Jinn	7	06.45	07.30	09.30
2	Jake Lloyd	Anakin	4	08.15	09.00	10.00
3	Natalie Portman	Queen Amidala	6	07.30	08.15	09.30
5	Ewan McGregor	Obi-Wan Kenobi	5	07.05	07.45	09.30
8	Hugh Quarshie	Captain Panaka	3	07.15	07.45	09.30
9	Christina Di Silva	Rabe	T 1	07.00	07.45	09.30
10	Friday Wilson	Eirtae	T 1	07.25	07.45	09.30
11	Ian McDiarmid	Palpatine	2	06.20	07.00	08.30
14	Terence Stamp	Valorum	1	06.45	07.30	08.30
44	Kenny Baker	R2 D2	T 2		08.00	09.30
47	Ahmed Best	Jar Jar	T 3	07.40	08.15	09.30
68	Keira Knightley	Sabe	T 4	07.30	09.00	10.00
STAND INS						
	Gavin Hale	Utility/Qui Gon				08.00
	Steve Ricard	Utility/Obi Wan				08.00
	Joan Field	Utility/Queen				08.00
	Ray Griffiths	Utility/Anakin				08.00
	Paul Kite	Utility				08.00
	Alan Harris	Utility/Valorum				08.00
CHAPERONES						
	Lisa Lloyd	For Jake Lloyd				09.00
	Carman Knightley	For Keira Knightley				09.00
CROWD (Total: 28)						
	1 man (C. dept)	Alien Taxi Driver			07.30	08.30
	4 men	Naboo Footsoldiers	1		06.30	08.30
	8 men	Coruscant Guard			07.30	08.30
	6 men	Ground crew			07.00	08.30
	2 men	Naboo Officers			07.00	08.30
	4 men	Naboo Guards			06.30	09.30
	3 men	Pilots			06.30	08.30
REQUIREMENTS						

ART DEPARTMENT: As per Gavin Bocquet. Coruscant taxi to move
PROPS: As per Ty Teiger and Peter Walpole
CAMERA: Giraffe crane. Additional grip Dave Cross
SPECIAL EFFECTS: R2D2 unit on wheels. Wind effect req.
MAKE-UP/HAIR: 1 additional hairdresser required
PRODUCTION: Tutor, Wendy Fletcher at studio fro Keira Knightley. School room on 1st floor
2 x Cast green room trailers & 1 x make/up,hair, wardrobe double under outside FS1a.
Crowd holding area & dressing area for cast on stage
FITTINGS: Crowd fittings (Human & Alien pod crew) from 2pm
CAST TRAVEL: Arrivals: Pernilla August (Shmi)
CATERING: Breakfast available in canteen from 7.00am. AM & PM breaks on set for 100 people

Left: The call sheet for the first day of filming with the full cast assembled.
Bottom left: Lucas with Jake Lloyd. Finding a young actor to portray the gifted and mysterious Anakin Skywalker had been the most challenging aspect of the casting process.

Best, who would provide the performance for the CG character of Jar Jar Binks. On the set, Lucas and the other actors relied heavily on Best to work out the timings, humor, interaction, and subtleties of character that otherwise would have had to wait until months later, when the computer-animated creature was inserted into the scenes. Through Best, Jar Jar was right there as a fully developed character even as cameras rolled—a big advantage in shooting the scenes, since Jar Jar was not only a major character with a great deal of screen time, but also a comic sidekick whose interactions with other actors in the scene was crucial.

"Usually in these situations," McCallum said, "you have nonactor stand-ins who are stiff and don't really give a performance. They're just bodies standing in for the CG characters. But with Ahmed and the other voice actors on the set, it really gave the other actors performances to work off of. George would rehearse the scene with

Right: Though his physical
presence would not be seen
in the final film, Ahmed
Best performed the role of
Jar Jar on the set to enable
the principal actors to work
out actions, comedic tim-
ings, and interactions with
the character.
Below: Lucas discusses an
upcoming scene with Natalie
Portman as Queen Amidala.

who they were talking to and what was going
on in the scene. And it also gave us perfect
reference for ILM when it came time to do
the Jar Jar computer-animated character."

On their first day of active duty, the
principals arrived at the studio at 7 A.M. for
makeup, hair, and costume preparations. As
the actors were readied, David Tattersall lit
the day's set—the Senate landing platform—with doubles standing in for the
actors. By 9 A.M., the actors arrived on set,
ready to enact the scene in which the
Queen's party arrives at Coruscant and is met
by Chancellor Valorum. Again, bluescreens
surrounded the practical landing platform;
ILM would insert magical Coruscant vistas
into the areas of blue in postproduction.

"Our very first scene involved coming
down the platform to meet Valorum," Liam
Neeson recalled. "Ewan and I were just
thrilled. We kept laughing and shouting:
'Yeeeahh! We're in *Star Wars*!'" Neeson's first
day also included a scene with Jake Lloyd, in
which the boy's high midi-chlorian count is

Ahmed, for example, and then he'd shoot one
or two takes with Ahmed in the scene. Then
he'd remove him and shoot the scene again;
but by this time, the actors were accustomed
to how the scene was supposed to go,
because they'd had their rehearsals with
Ahmed. The fact that Jar Jar wasn't there
didn't throw them. The actors understood

discussed and the nature of midi-chlorians explained. "The scene had a lot of scientific dialogue, and George had to explain what it all meant and the theory behind it. He said that we all have thousands of bacteria in our systems—suppose a particular strain had a life force that was connected to the universe? And what if some people had a stronger strain of these bacteria than others did? I thought the idea was both fascinating and believable."

Perhaps the most character-driven scene in the entire film—the dinner meeting between Qui-Gon, Padmé, Jar Jar, Anakin, and Shmi within the slave quarters—was shot just days later. Situated two weeks into the shooting schedule, the scene benefited from the fact that the actors had broken the ice with each other and with Lucas. "There are basically two ways to approach working with actors," Lucas asserted. "One is more 'method,' more acting-class oriented, where you are intimately involved with the actors

on a personal, as well as a professional, level. I prefer the traditional way of working, which you find more in Europe, and in England, especially. There, it is exclusively a professional collaboration. The director says, 'This is what I want you to do; this is where I want you to go.' It isn't about trying to find the motivation for every moment. I'm not like some directors who will sit for days and analyze what is going on. In the case of this film, if an actor had a specific question, it was easy for me to give them a quick answer. And if an actor made a suggestion about the character, I could immediately decide if it was appropriate or not.

"But I don't think that actors should necessarily know everything about the character in order for them to play their parts. They need to know enough to give the character the right feel, the right look, the right persona. On *The Empire Strikes Back*, for example, Mark Hamill didn't know until the day the scene was shot that Darth Vader was Luke's father. It wasn't important for him to know that until his character found out. I felt that if he had known about it, it would have changed and complicated the way he approached the role."

Left: Hairstylist Sarah Love attends to actress Natalie Portman for her transformation into Padmé the hand-maiden.
Below: Lucas and Liam Neeson confer regarding the next shot.

Far right: Security on the set was so tight, everyone was required to wear a name tag—even Lucas.
Below and bottom: The dinner scene in Anakin's hovel was energized by the subtle chemistry between Qui-Gon and Shmi—and by Jar Jar's odd table manners.

The dinner scene—and in fact all the scenes featuring interchange between Qui-Gon and Shmi—was energized by a subtle chemistry between the two characters. "There is just a hint of romance in those encounters," Liam Neeson said, "something very subtle. Both Pernilla and I were very conscious of that. There was warmth between them when they looked at each other. It didn't have to be obvious, just subtle and loving."

After four weeks at Leavesden, the cast and crew moved to Reggia Palace at Caserta, Italy, where they would spend the next several days shooting interiors of the Naboo palace in Theed. Many of Natalie Portman's scenes as Queen Amidala would be filmed that week; and while there, the actress sprained her ankle—causing her to have to

be left behind for one more day when the company moved to Tunisia.

In Tunisia, the production would spend two weeks filming Mos Espa exteriors. Just transplanting the production to the site was an enormous task. With film equipment, sets, props, costumes, and Podracers all required on location, fifty tons of material had to be shipped to the site. "The most challenging aspect of shooting on location is moving," Rick McCallum asserted. "You are basically moving an entire village—your crew, all the pots and pans, clothes, and everything else that has to do with creating life." Spotting an ad in a magazine for a big Russian freight plane, McCallum hit on the idea of chartering one of the giant aircraft to move his "village" to Tunisia. "I told George that we could save a lot of money by loading up everything in one of those planes, which are the biggest cargo planes in the world—and he went for it."

The production office was set up at the Palm Beach Hotel in Tozeur, Tunisia, at the edge of the Sahara Desert. However, the sets representing the streets of Mos Espa, the Podrace arena, and Anakin's slave quarters on Tatooine were re-created north of the city, in the middle of the desert. The sets were made of a wooden frame, covered in wire mesh and sculpted foam. "We built Mos Espa with local labor and material to get the

Above: After four weeks at Leavesden, the cast and crew moved to Italy for the Naboo palace interiors. Below: The next stop was Tunisia, where all the exterior Tatooine sequences were filmed.

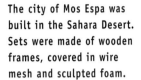
The city of Mos Espa was built in the Sahara Desert. Sets were made of wooden frames, covered in wire mesh and sculpted foam.

feel of North African architecture," Bocquet recalled.

True to the overall production mandate to save money by building only what was needed, the Mos Espa sets were built up to the heights of the actors or a bit higher. "None of those sets had tops," Rick McCallum said. "We knew what we needed. But if George decided, at the last minute, that he wanted to tilt up more, we'd just slap up bluescreen so ILM could fill in the sets digitally. We had twelve hundred and fifty yards of bluescreen that we owned, so we could use it whenever and however we wanted. We had portable bluescreens, miniature bluescreens—they were with us wherever we went, and they could go up in literally minutes. They gave us a lot of freedom, and we saved an absolute fortune in set construction."

The heat in the Sahara Desert in late July would prove to be the most challenging aspect of the Tunisia shoot. Daily call sheets warned, "Please take care in the sun. Drink plenty of water and rehydrate. Wear a hat, stay in the shade." It was a warning not to be taken lightly in a locale where summer temperatures could easily top 130 degrees.

The heat was particularly problematic for Nick Dudman and his makeup effects crew, as well as for those unfortunate souls wearing the rubbery masks and suits created for the aliens walking the streets of Mos Espa. Foam latex heads were equipped with their own cooling devices and sand filters; but even so, time spent in the masks and heads had to be kept to a minimum. "The trick was to have the extras rehearse their scenes without their heads on," Nick Dudman observed. "When we were ready to shoot the scene, we'd put the heads on and keep the extras under an umbrella, with plenty of water available, until the cameras started rolling.

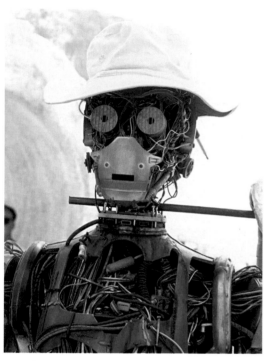

If an extra started to feel very uncomfortable, we'd just stop shooting." At the end of each day, the foam latex heads were fumigated and sprayed with disinfectant, then numbered so that they would be assigned to the same performers the following morning.

Special "cool suits" were also rented for the shoot. Cold water was continually pumped through tubes mounted inside the vests, which kept body temperatures down and allowed actors such as Ahmed Best to wear heavy costumes in the hot weather for a longer period of time. Air-conditioned vehicles were also used for storing film stock. "I was afraid the whole time there that the film would warp," David Tattersall said. "We had a routine where we would take the film out of the air-conditioning and put it immediately in the shade for a short period of time before we actually needed it."

Even with special equipment and air-conditioning at their disposal, however, the cast and crew found the Tunisia shoot to be trying. "Working in the desert was very diffi-

Top left and bottom right: The desert heat was especially brutal for performers in heavy costumes and rubbery masks who played background aliens in street and Podrace scenes.
Above left: C-3PO wears a hat as protection against the desert sun.
Top right: Extras made up as aliens wait to be filmed as spectators at the Podrace.

92

cult," Lucas admitted. "The heat was draining. I tried to be conscious of how everyone was holding up—especially Jake. He would never tell me if he was having a problem. So I'd check with his mother; and there were a few times when he really needed a rest. But as difficult as it was, Tunisia was the place that brought back the most memories for me. It looks like Tatooine—it must be *Star Wars*!"

Professionalism and dedication ultimately pulled everyone through the grueling experience. "The worst part of making this film was the heat in Tunisia," Liam Neeson conceded. "But we'd all look at George, in his blue jeans, totally unfazed by it all, and we thought, 'If our governor is not complaining, we certainly shouldn't.'"

Ahmed Best's antics both in front of the camera and behind the scenes also helped to distract the cast and crew. "He kept us laughing," Natalie Portman recalled. "Even though he was the one who was the most uncomfortable—since he had to wear this full rubber suit—he never complained. He just kept making jokes."

Even more devastating than the heat—at least temporarily—was a storm that threatened the entire production. At dinner one evening, Lucas spotted dark, ominous clouds off in the distance. "It didn't look good to me," Lucas recalled. "I had been through the same experience on the first *Star Wars*—it was as if the storm had hidden away for twenty years, just waiting to come back! When we started to hear thunder, I asked Rick McCallum, 'What are we going to do tomorrow?' And he said, 'Don't worry—we'll shoot!' But he was being optimistic."

That optimism proved unfounded when, at midnight, a storm hit the area with tremendous force. "It was like a hurricane and a tornado combined," McCallum recalled. At risk were equipment and all the Mos Espa exterior sets that had been erected in the desert during the past twelve weeks. Determined to see how the sets were faring, McCallum and production supervisor David Brown jumped into a four-wheel-drive vehicle and got as far as the edge of the desert. "It was terrifying. Wind was hitting my car so hard, I thought we were going to be turned over. So we went back to the hotel

and just waited. When the storm let up a bit, I went back out to the sets—or what was left of them." By three o'clock that morning, George Lucas got the call he'd been dreading. Not only were the sets gone, the crew could not get back into the location.

Hours later, when the crew could return to inspect the damage, they were devastated by its extent. Mos Espa looked as if it had been hit by a tornado. Costumes, wigs, tents, Podracers, even buildings were scattered, turned over, destroyed. Only one set was still standing—the landing ramp of the Queen's ship, the only part of the ship to be erected in the desert—and the shooting schedule was quickly rearranged to accommodate filming of that set's scenes. "That

ramp for the ship was the one thing that saved us," McCallum said, "because it was the only thing that hadn't been destroyed in the storm. If we hadn't had that, we'd have been in real trouble. But because that stood, we were able to shoot there while the other sets were being reconstructed."

As Lucas continued to shoot on the ship's platform, McCallum and David Brown organized the crew to rebuild the damaged sets at a frenetic pace. Fourteen hundred costumes had to be dug out of the sand and cleaned. New equipment had to be brought in to replace what had been destroyed, lost, or irrevocably damaged. Every department pitched in, and even the Tunisian army arrived to rebuild the streets of Mos Espa.

When a violent storm destroyed most of the Mos Espa sets, the entire crew pitched in to repair the damage. Despite the calamity, production continued without losing a day of shooting.

Above: The new R2-D2 model was fitted with all-terrain wheels that enabled it to maneuver over the rough desert landscape. Behind R2-D2, George Lucas uses old technology to eliminate tracks in the sand.
Far right: McCallum and Lucas on location in Tunisia.
Right: Lucas directs Jake Lloyd for an upcoming desert scene.

"We managed to rebuild," McCallum said, "without losing a day of shooting. We would literally finish painting a set, and immediately bring in the actors to start filming. In fact, in a couple of scenes, Natalie walked in and suddenly realized that her shoes were stuck to the paint!"

Remarkably, despite the disaster, Episode I was still on schedule as the Tunisia shoot wrapped in the middle of August. "Tunisia was pure adrenaline," McCallum commented, "and the shoot there was fantastic, despite the problems we had to face. There was a volatility about it that was unnerving, yet exhilarating."

The crew returned to Leavesden where, for the next six weeks, the remainder of the film's interiors would be shot. In the first unit's absence, Bocquet's team had replaced the original sets with interiors of the Queen's spacecraft, Theed interiors, the Jedi Council chamber, and the generator room where Qui-Gon and Obi-Wan square off with Darth Maul in a spectacular lightsaber battle.

After a week on stage, the company moved to a nearby forest—Whippendell Wood—to shoot exteriors of the Naboo swamp and the Gungan sacred temple ruins. Both settings would be extended considerably through miniatures and digital matte paintings.

With the return to Leavesden Studios, the crew shot the Jedi Council scenes. The temple set was built on platforms to accommodate puppeteers stationed below.

Two weeks into the final leg of production, Lucas filmed scenes in the Jedi Council chamber, including Qui-Gon's introduction of Anakin to the council, Anakin's test scene, and the scene in which the council announces its decision that the boy is too old to be disciplined in the ways of the Force. The Jedi Council was made up of humanoid members, played by actors wearing prosthetic makeups; outlandish alien characters, realized through animatronic puppets; and humans, such as Mace Windu, portrayed by Samuel L. Jackson.

But the most prominent character in the council scenes was Yoda, the beloved Jedi Master first introduced in *The Empire Strikes Back*. Just as he had done for that film, Frank Oz—a successful director in his own right—provided both the voice and the performance for Yoda, expertly manipulating the puppet built by Nick Dudman. Neither Lucas nor McCallum had ever considered attempt-

ing to reintroduce the character of Yoda without Frank Oz as the man behind the puppet. "I'd been speaking to Frank about it off and on for two or three years before we did the movie," McCallum said. "There was just no way we were going to do it without him. We fit our schedule around his. He'd just finished a movie, and he fit us in for two days between the completion of his movie and the start of his press conferences. Two days and he was gone. But it was essential to have him there. Yoda would not be Yoda without Frank Oz."

After two decades, Oz still recalls seeing the first drawing of Yoda. "As soon as I saw it," Oz related, "I felt very strongly about the character, about his power, his wisdom, and his humanity. I liked the paradox of a powerful, all-knowing fellow who looked old and weak." The character, as seen in Episode I, is younger and, perhaps, less weak—but still as challenging to puppeteer. "From a physical standpoint, Yoda is very demanding, but I'm always happy to revisit the character and to work with George."

Since multiple performers were required to bring Yoda to life, Oz worked in tandem

Right: Anakin undergoes testing by the Jedi Council
Below: Qui-Gon tells the Jedi Council he fears his attacker on Tatooine was a Sith Lord.
The panoramic vistas of Coruscant seen from the Council's windows would be added in post-production.

with puppeteers Kathy Smee, Don Austen, and David Greenaway. With the exception of one CG shot near the end of the film that would show the Jedi Master walking, Yoda's entire performance was created by Oz and this team of puppeteers, each of whom articulated one particular feature of the puppet.

Greenaway had operated Yoda's eyes for *Return of the Jedi* and was called back to repeat his performance for Episode I, manipulating radio controls from off camera. Austen radio-controlled other facial features. Smee articulated Yoda's right arm, working alongside Frank Oz from beneath the council chamber set. But while Yoda was a team effort, the heart of the character's performance came from Frank Oz. "Frank *is* the character," Smee commented. "We just tried to give him freedom, and to work with his performance, to flow with it. No matter what we rehearsed, Frank would always do something a little more, a little different for the real take."

"We could see what Yoda was doing on TV monitors beneath the set," Oz elaborated. "If George was satisfied with a take, we'd move on. Other times, we'd play back the performance and decide to make some adjustments."

Despite the fact that Yoda was made of

silicone and radio control mechanisms, the character was as real as any other. George Lucas directed Yoda just as he directed all the actors on the set. "Acting is acting," Lucas stated, "whether it is a human actor, a CG character, or a puppet. It's all the same. Most people think of Yoda as being real, because he is the height of puppet artistry. After Frank Oz did *Empire*, I tried to get him nominated for an Academy Award; but we heard back that puppetry wasn't an art. *I* think it is an art—and Yoda represents the highest level of that art."

The actors, too, reacted to Yoda as if he were a living, breathing character. "The way Yoda came to life on the set was really special," Samuel L. Jackson observed. "George would say, 'Action,' and Yoda was suddenly just *there*, doing his scene. And then George would say, 'Cut,' Frank Oz would take his hand out, and Yoda would slump over as if he was hungover or not feeling well. And you felt like, 'Man, somebody help Yoda!'"

"The actors were so taken by Yoda," Oz added, "it was extraordinary. I was very flattered. I think people respond to this character because he is very much like a Zen mas-

ter—and I think everyone would love to have someone like him to talk to. Yoda is universally appealing."

One of the last sequences to be shot was the long lightsaber battle between Qui-Gon, Obi-Wan, and Darth Maul, which takes place within the power generator complex of the Theed hangar. The sword fight had been roughed out in an animatic created by Ben Burtt in preproduction. Since Lucas had suggested a martial arts influence in the fight scene, Burtt had studied footage featuring interesting and inspiring swordplay, martial arts, and acrobatics. "I cut together some of this martial arts footage," Burtt explained, "and from that began to develop a style of how the Jedi would fight."

Working from those animatics, stunt coordinator Nick Gillard choreographed the battle, as well as all the movie's action scenes. Gillard's journey into the world of film stunts was an interesting one. After running away from military school at the age of twelve, he joined the circus. By the age of sixteen, he had become a world-class horse trick rider. His first stunt work was on the remake of *The Thief of Baghdad*, and he has

Left: Samuel L. Jackson as Council member Mace Windu.
Below: Lucas with stunt coordinator Nick Gillard.

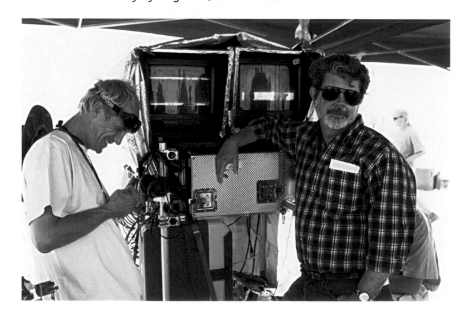

Right: Gillard, who would choreograph the lightsaber battles, confers with Ray Park as Darth Maul.
Below: Ewan McGregor and a stuntman portraying the fallen Qui-Gon rehearse the climactic lightsaber duel with Gillard standing in for Ray Park. Gillard took inspiration from fencing, kendo, tennis, and even tree chopping to create dynamic battle moves.

since distinguished himself by setting two unofficial world records: one for a power boat jump performed on the film *Amsterdamned*, and another for a two-minute full fire burn without air for *Alien 3*. Gillard also worked on the original *Star Wars* trilogy. More than thirty-five films

and twenty years later, his career came full circle with Episode I. He started the assignment by reading the script and studying the storyboards, noting what each stunt should look like and how it might be done.

Among the most challenging of those stunt sequences was the lightsaber duel, which would be the most dynamic, most acrobatic fight in the history of the *Star Wars* saga. "I was looking for a kind of sword fighting that was reminiscent of what had been done in the previous films," George Lucas explained, "but also something that was more energized. Up to this point, we had never actually seen a real Jedi in action. We'd seen old men, young boys, and characters who were half droid–half man, but we'd never seen a Jedi in his prime. I wanted to do that with a fight that was faster and more dynamic—and we were able to pull that off. Nick Gillard did a great job, and the actors really got into it."

To design the exciting Jedi choreography

Neeson and McGregor worked long hours with Gillard to learn and execute the lightsaber battle with Darth Maul.
Below right: George Lucas offers some tips of his own.

Lucas envisioned, Gillard studied fencing, kendo, tennis, and even tree chopping. After the style and choreography had been determined, he worked long hours with Liam Neeson, Ewan McGregor, and Ray Park to create the lightsaber duel. "We were really lucky," Gillard noted, "because both Liam and Ewan were exceptional—and they had to be, because they were doing most of their own stunts. Having them do the battle only added to the sequence, because no one understood these characters better than they did. They were also as fast as any of the stunt guys they would be fighting in the movie."

Neither Neeson nor McGregor had ever been required to perform such a long, complicated, taxing stunt sequence. "I had done

Right: Though the actors performed much of the battle themselves, acrobatic feats such as high jumps and somersaults were executed by stunt people. One exception was Ray Park, the actor portraying Darth Maul, who is also a stuntman. Pneumatic ramps were used to catapult stunt performers into the air.

Below: Lucas with second unit director Roger Christian, who worked alongside the main unit to ensure the tremendous shot load was completed by the end of the shooting schedule.

some fighting at drama school," McGregor said, "but never anything that physical."

The fight was so long and complex, in fact, the actors learned and then performed only a few moves at a time. Those bits and pieces would then be assembled into a complete sequence in editing. "I was amazed by Ewan's ability to remember all the moves," Neeson recalled. "I had trouble remembering two or three moves at a time, but he could do twelve, thirteen moves, having just learned them. Fortunately, George gave us the time to get comfortable with the scene, and eventually it got done."

The swordplay was enhanced considerably by the fact that Ray Park was a real stuntman and a fencing expert. "In addition," Gillard noted, "Ray is trained in five or six martial arts, and he is a really good gymnast."

"Ray really knew what he was doing," Lucas added, "and his presence and expertise motivated the other actors, as well."

The actors were also motivated by the sheer power of holding a lightsaber—one of the most recognizable and iconic weapons ever conceived. "Before we started shooting," Liam Neeson recalled, "George showed up with a huge gilded box. In it were lightsabers, and he asked me to pick one. I chose one, and he said, 'That's yours now.' It was quite a moment. And I did get to keep it—it was mounted for me at the end of the film. I was thrilled."

Gillard contributed to the construction of the lightsabers, which were made of resin, wood, and aluminum tubing that would be replaced by the visual effects to create a lightsaber glow. During fight tests, Gillard—who was, above all else, responsible for the safety of each stunt—detected small bits of shrapnel flying from the props when the blades clashed. To remedy the potential safety hazard, the sabers were shrink-wrapped in plastic. Twenty swords a day were usually required when an action sequence was being shot. Three hundred lightsaber blades total were used during filming.

In addition to sophisticated sword fighting, the fight sequence—which would take nearly a month to shoot—featured an incredible variety of jumps, somersaults, and other acrobatic feats. Typically, stunt jumps are achieved by suspending stuntmen or actors on wires, which are then removed digitally from the footage. But Gillard looked for a more dynamic approach for Episode I. "I just didn't like wires," Gillard explained. "I never thought the moves on wires looked

believable. Instead, we used nitrogen air rams." Stuntmen would stand on platforms attached to the pneumatic rams; and as the air pressure was released, they would be catapulted into the air. "With air rams, the performers looked as if they were flying, and the landings were hard and realistic. With wires, they looked like they were floating through the air. It wasn't as powerful a move." Park executed one of the most impressive stunts—an aerial backward somersault, traveling forty feet across the stage.

For the most part, such action and stunt sequences were filmed by the second unit crew. Second unit director Roger Christian had worked as a set decorator on the original *Star Wars* and had received an Oscar for his contribution. Now an established film director (*Nostradamus*), Christian nevertheless welcomed the opportunity to serve as second unit director for Episode I.

Typically, second unit will shoot pickups and inserts after the main unit has completed a particular shot. But Episode I was such a huge production, and the number of shots and setups per day so ambitious, Christian and his crews worked right alongside the

Producer Rick McCallum strove to create an atmosphere of calm on the set, despite a demanding and hectic schedule.

main unit, picking up shots that had fallen through the cracks due to the frenetic pace. His role required Christian to thoroughly understand what Lucas wanted in each and every shot. "I'd observe George as he was shooting his scenes," Christian said. "And then he would walk me through each of the shots I was going to pick up, telling me how he saw them."

By the time the shoot had ended—on September 30, 1997—twenty-five hundred first-unit camera setups and twelve hundred second-unit shots had been realized in just over three months. It was an ambitious pace for moviemaking, with two to three times the standard number of setups completed each and every day. Yet, remarkably, an atmosphere of calm was maintained on the set throughout the hectic schedule. "You never heard anyone screaming on the set," Rick McCallum noted. "Even if we had last-minute changes—which a film always has—our crew didn't look at it as a problem. Instead, they saw those things as challenges; and for this crew, challenges were seen not only as fun, but as a way of saying to George, 'Go ahead, throw anything at us, we're ready to do anything for you.'"

PART 3

"I could do whatever I wanted."

While story and characters were the primary elements that contributed to the original trilogy's success, all three films also featured stunning visuals, created through effects that were, at the time, groundbreaking. But as much as the world marveled at the spectacle, Lucas had been frustrated by the limitations of visual effects technology, and how those limitations negatively impacted his storytelling. "When I wrote the first scripts," Lucas recalled, "it was very difficult, because there were a lot of things I *wanted* to do that I couldn't do, because of the technology. It was frustrating, but I did the best I could at the time."

In fact, Lucas's long-held frustration with the state of technology and how it limited his ability to create an entire world was, in large part, the reason behind his long delay in producing the new trilogy of films. "I didn't want to go back and write one of these movies unless I had the technology available to really tell the kind of story I was interested in telling. I wanted to be able to explore the world I'd created to its fullest potential. So I waited until I had the technological means to do that."

Proof that the time had come was delivered in the form of Steven Spielberg's *Jurassic Park*, a film that featured photorealistic dinosaurs created by ILM through computer animation. That watershed film, which marked the beginning of a new age in effects, was released in 1993. By 1994, George Lucas and crew were hard at work on Episode I. "Writing the script was much more enjoyable this time around," stated Lucas, "because I wasn't constrained by anything. I didn't have to say to myself, 'Well, I can't have one of these creatures, because there's no way to do it with a guy in a suit.' You can't write one of these movies without knowing how you're going to accomplish it. With CG at my disposal, I knew I could do whatever I wanted."

By 1997—the year the *Special Edition* movies were released—digital technology had developed considerably, in large part through the efforts of Lucas himself. Finally, Lucas had at his disposal effects techniques that would enable him to make the original films "right"—or at least edge them closer to his original vision. But the *Special Edition* films were not only an opportunity for Lucas to go back and repair the past. In large part, the *Special Edition* releases of *Star Wars*, *The Empire Strikes Back*, and *Return of the Jedi* were testing grounds for how computer-generated effects might be applied to the new trilogy of films. "Through the *Special Editions*," Lucas said, "I was able to test things and make sure that I could actually pull off the things that I wanted to pull off

Opposite page: The inimitable Jar Jar Binks. Jar Jar is the most expressive, complex computer-generated character ever created.

in this movie. I tested a lot of ideas, and I learned a lot through the process. And by the time the *Special Edition* movies were released, I was convinced I could do everything I wanted."

Digital technology, as well as other effects techniques, would play a more prominent role in the new *Star Wars* film than any in history. Out of the completed film's twenty-two hundred shots, nineteen hundred of those would be, in whole or in part, effects shots. *Titanic*, an extremely ambitious visual effects film, had featured a total of five hundred effects shots—a count that rose to nine hundred when wire-removals and other digital tweaks were included. At double that number of effects, Episode I would be a visual effects achievement of unprecedented scale.

The assignment was so enormous, in fact, that three visual effects supervisors, as opposed to the standard single supervisor, would work on the show, dividing the workload among them. First on the production was John Knoll, who served as the on-set supervisor during production, then oversaw the Podrace and space battle sequences in

the postproduction phase. Supervising the underwater sequence on Naboo—which included the submarine scenes, the sea monsters, and the city of Otoh Gunga—was Dennis Muren, the winner of eight Academy Awards for visual effects and a veteran of films such as the original *Star Wars* trilogy, the *Indiana Jones* trilogy, *The Abyss*, *Terminator 2: Judgment Day*, *Jurassic Park*, and its sequel, *The Lost World*. Muren would also supervise the massive ground battle between the Gungans and the Trade Federation droid army at the film's climax. Finally, supervisor Scott Squires took on the lightsaber effects, the long battle in the generator complex, and digital shots of Theed. Squires was another longtime ILM veteran and had supervised the effects for *Dragonheart*, which had featured some of the most complex character-driven computer animation created up to that time. Working in cooperation with all three units was ILM model-shop supervisor Steve Gawley and his miniatures team, as well as digital effects animation director Rob Coleman, who was in charge of all the film's computer-generated character animation.

Above left: Chrissie England, ILM's visual effects executive producer.
Above right: Digital model supervisor Geoff Campbell.

In postproduction, characters such as Jar Jar were animated, then composited into live-action plates shot during principal photography.
Below: Jar Jar was inserted in this scene where he first meets Qui-Gon and Obi-Wan.
Bottom: Jar Jar on the streets of Mos Espa.

While the bulk of ILM's work would be done in postproduction, after principal photography had wrapped, the company had been involved, at least tangentially, from the very beginning. Storyboards and animatics created by the crew at Skywalker Ranch in the two years before filming started were turned over to ILM as soon as they were completed, as was the finalized script. "By that time," Lucas said, "we had designed most of the characters ILM would be producing through CG. We had models of Jar Jar, Watto, and the different droids, which ILM used to start building their computer mod-

els. As soon as we finished filming, we began cutting sequences without the effects, then turning those cut scenes over to ILM. Ultimately, they had the whole movie to work from."

To prepare for the assignment, ILM initiated a research and development effort on behalf of Episode I even as the movie was being shot in England. One of the problems that had to be solved during that period was how to create computer-generated clothing—how to simulate, with computer graphics, the look and flowing dynamics of fabric hanging from CG characters such as Jar Jar

others, as needed. In some cases, the scanning of a maquette was skipped altogether, and computer models were built from scratch, patch by patch.

Senior digital model supervisor Geoff Campbell and a modeling team of eighteen started working on the show as early as 1996, initially concentrating their efforts on Jar Jar, the most complex and most prominent CG character in the movie. Campbell started by studying Terryl Whitlatch's drawings of the character, then building a rough mock-up in the computer to test the range of expression allowed by the design. "Traditionally," Campbell said, "we would build a maquette or clay model of the character first, then scan that into the computer and build the CG model from there. But in this case, we didn't want to finalize Jar Jar's design until we knew what range of expressions he could make. We wanted to be able to change the design somewhat, if the animation required it."

In this early stage of development, Jar Jar had a cartoony look and style of behavior. "He was very flexible," Campbell said. "His eyes could protrude six to ten inches off his head, and he had a smile that could pull all the way to one side. But that was too unrealistic. We had to pull back from that and try to make him a more believable character. For any digital character, you have to create an anatomy that fits the character but is also believable."

Once a more refined model was built, Campbell created a library of expressions, suggested by Ahmed Best's performance. With this library of expressions available, animators could create Jar Jar's performance much more efficiently, using an appropriate expression for each moment, rather than animating an expression from scratch every time it was required. In general, lip syncing

Each CG character first had to be created as a computer model. Scaled maquettes of characters were built, scanned into the computer to provide a basic shape, then modeled in more detail by CG modelers at ILM. Here, sculptor Mark Siegel works on a maquette of Watto the junk dealer.

Binks. "We were also going to be creating more digital environments than we'd ever done before," ILM executive producer Chrissie England recalled. "So while the shoot was going on, there was a lot of technology that still had to be developed. We used the time to do a lot of testing of different techniques so we'd be up and ready when the shots actually started coming in."

The film's preproduction and production periods were also used to build the two hundred twenty-five computer models for all the CG characters that would be featured in the movie. Typically, computer models would be built by scanning in a maquette—a small-scale model of a given character—which would result in a three-dimensional, wireframe form made up of many patches of points. The model then would be refined by the digital modeler, who would add points for more detailed areas, deleting them in

Watto's initial design was modified when ILM animators discovered the original shape of the character's muzzle area and trunk made lip-sync nearly impossible. In his final design, Watto spoke from the side of his mouth.

and facial expressions were designed by observing photographs, other people, and even one's own expressions in a mirror. In fact, as he worked, Campbell had two mirrors next to him at all times so that he could study his own lip and facial movements. This common practice resulted in CG characters that, in some cases, bore a fleeting resemblance to the model supervisor in charge of their facial expression design.

The animators also used the facial library as a tool to make their characters look as if they were saying the appropriate lines of dialogue. "We create what is called

in traditional animation a 'model sheet,'" Campbell explained. "It is a facial library in which the animators can go in and get whatever expression they need for their lip-sync lines. They end up taking the opening and closing of the character's jaw, and blending that with whatever expression is appropriate for the dialogue." All the other Gungans were built by modifying the Jar Jar model—although the characters of Boss Nass and Captain Tarpals, both of whom had major speaking roles, required their own expression libraries.

One of the most difficult characters to model was Watto—in part, because his anatomical design was more whimsical than practical. The character had to be built and animated in such a way that the audience would believe Watto's tiny wings could actually keep his rotund body airborne. His facial configuration also complicated the creation of an expression library. "Doug Chiang designed Watto with two sets of long, almost walruslike tusks on either side of his trunk," Campbell explained. "Rob Coleman wanted the character to speak from the side of his mouth, because his trunk would have made it impossible to see him speak otherwise. But we couldn't figure out how to get his lips to close over the top of those tusks if he was saying the letter *m* for instance, or *b*. It was suggested we scale down the teeth; but Doug felt that they were an important part of Watto's character. A compromise was reached by breaking off one of the teeth and scaling back the others slightly. The chipped tooth worked fine for old Watto, and the lip sync was successful."

A certain amount of trial and error was also required for the Sebulba model, which went through various transformations and the hands of several different modelers before it was finalized. At the end of the character's evolution, Sebulba was more extreme behaviorally than initially intended, and the original set of expressions had to be expanded to accommodate his new, wider emotional range.

Completed CG character models were, at this point, stationary. Each was sent to the chaining department, where the underlying armatures that would determine movement were applied. Technical animation lead James Tooley and his group were responsible for the chaining, while Tim McLaughlin oversaw the enveloping, a technique whereby the movement of the character's "skin" over the underlying structure of the model is determined. Enveloping ensures that the surface of the model does not split as it is put through a range of motion. Both chaining and enveloping prepared the computer models for the animation department.

Finally, the models went to the Viewpaint team. Viewpaint, ILM's proprietary 3-D paint system, enables artists to add all the colors, textures, and surface details to the previously gray-shaded model. "My job is an extension of what Doug Chiang and his

Doug Chiang inspects the Sebulba maquette—in progress—with sculptor Richard Miller.

team do," Viewpaint supervisor Jean Bolte explained. "They come up with the original design, and produce it either as a detailed maquette or a sketch; and then we flesh that out to make it look absolutely believable."

As the CG models were painted, Rob Coleman and the animation department began bringing the characters to life, working with models that were in wire-frame or gray-shaded form. As the director of animation, Coleman would be the key to ensuring high-quality character animation and performance throughout. "This movie had a dozen *major* digital characters," Rick McCallum commented, "one of which would have ninety minutes of screen time! And they all had to be seamlessly integrated into the movie—absolutely spectacular and real. Rob Coleman was the guy behind that. He made sure that all of the CG characters delivered real performances. Each one of them was a really good, solid piece of acting."

Just as Geoff Campbell and the modelers had started with Jar Jar, the animation team also began with the character, which would require the most complex and extensive animation of any in the movie. "Jar Jar was a

for the character's personality and behavior was Ahmed Best's performance in the film. Lucas intended to incorporate that performance—the looseness of his body, the way he walked, his comic timing—into the CG character, and yet take it to an extreme. In Lucas's mind, Jar Jar had to be even more rubbery and more fluid and more "otherworldly" than what an actor had been able to achieve on the set. In addition, Lucas suggested that Coleman think of a Buster Keaton–type character when animating Jar Jar. "As soon as I heard that," Coleman recalled, "I immediately understood the direction George wanted to go with Jar Jar. George approached most of the other characters the same way."

Boss Nass's animation relied most heavily on Brian Blessed's vocal performance. "Brian Blessed brought so much to the character, we hardly needed other references for Boss Nass," Coleman observed. Similarly, Andrew Secombe's vocal performance for Watto was extremely helpful in developing

Above: Viewpaint supervisor Jean Bolte at work on a Sebulba bust. Using Viewpaint, ILM's computer paint system, Bolte would replicate the sculpture's paint scheme on the computer model of the character.
Below: Animation supervisor Rob Coleman oversaw the performances of literally hundreds of computer-animated characters.

leading character," Coleman said, "the main sidekick. But even though he was a CG character, he had to look every bit as realistic as Chewbacca did in the early films."

After reading the script and meeting with Lucas to discuss performance issues, Coleman put together a personality profile for Jar Jar. The first and foremost reference

111

Top: A final composite consisting of live-action footage of Liam Neeson and Ewan McGregor, along with a CG element of Jar Jar in the Gungan submarine, in front of a computer generated background. ILM technical directors took great pains to light their CG characters so they would integrate convincingly into live-action plates.
Left: A composite shot in a scene between Qui-Gon and Watto, in Watto's salvage yard.

that character's animation. Lucas had described Watto as a sleazy car dealer, a pirate, a gambler. "I also asked George if Watto was from Tatooine," Coleman recalled, "because it was important to find out if he would be comfortable in the heat. George said that, yes, he was. Jar Jar, on the other hand, would be very uncomfortable in the desert, since he was from an underwater world. Incorporating those kinds of behavioral details brought richness and a higher level of believability to the animation."

Sebulba's history was crucial to developing his animation. "We thought of him as the greatest racer who ever lived," Coleman said. "By understanding his identity and his backstory, we were better able to design his physical behavior and overall attitude."

The Podrace sequence, which would feature both puppet and CG racers, gave the animation team the opportunity to create a wide range of characters. Ben Quadinaros

Shots from the Podrace sequence. A variety of wild-looking alien Podrace drivers, including Sebulba (above) and Gasgano (right), were computer generated for the showcase sequence.

was animated as a comedic character—a big, dim, eternally inept racer who always enters, but rarely gets off the ground. Gasgano was given spiderlike movement, facilitated by his many limbs. Ratts was seen as a mobster character, a New York mafioso who is tough, loud, and rude, while Teemto revealed bullying tendencies.

Not all of the CG characters were speaking roles; and in those cases, human-style personality traits were not as important as

basic issues of size, volume, speed, and movement. Creating the feeling of size was particularly vital in animating the three sea monsters featured in the underwater sequence on Naboo. "We were dealing with some really enormous characters in that sequence," Rob Coleman noted. "The sando aqua monster was supposed to be seven hundred and twenty feet long; and if we moved him too quickly, he wouldn't have that kind of scale. We had to be aware of his motion and how it impacted his scale. To get that right, we looked at whale footage, observing how they swim and move through the water."

A lead animator was assigned to each CG creature model: Lou Dellarosa headed the Jar Jar team; Linda Bel oversaw Watto; Hal Hickel was assigned Boss Nass; and Miguel Fuertes supervised Sebulba. By the time the project was in full swing, Rob Coleman and the animation leads were overseeing a team of forty-five animators. "It was a huge animation show," Coleman commented. "In fact, George once referred to Episode I as his first animated feature."

The final step in bringing the CG characters to life was to integrate them into the live-action plates, a job that fell to ILM's team of technical directors. TDs ensured that the lighting on the characters was consistent with that in the live-action, for example, and that the appropriate computer-generated shadows were cast from those characters.

Hard-surface models such as ships, tanks, and droids also had to be modeled and animated. Like the character models, most hard-surface computer models were built by first scanning practical versions from the ILM model shop. From there, the models went through much the same progression as the CG characters—Viewpainting, animation, and integration by a team of technical directors.

Droid animation, led by James Tooley, was expedited by the use of motion capture, a technique in which targets are placed on a special suit worn by a performer. By photographing the performer in movement, and feeding that data into a computer, the motion can be tracked through 3-D space, then interpolated in a CG form, seen on a monitor. The action can then be applied to a 3-D CG model. Coleman was one of the performers who submitted to the motion-capture drill. "They could film me walking with the motion capture cameras, and when that action was applied to a droid, it looked very mechanical," Coleman explained. "Since all the droids had to move exactly the same

Gungan leader Boss Nass was another computer generated character. Because the character wore a heavy cloak, the ILM crew had to develop a cloth simulator that would make the article of clothing move and flow with the dynamics of real fabric.

way, motion capture was the ideal technique."

Shots of spacecraft seen in the final space battle would be realized with both 3-D computer models and practical models shot using motion control. The sequence was so complex, however, and some of the shots so fleeting, John Knoll determined fairly early on that he could produce a great number of 2-D shots quickly and inexpensively, using low-resolution models.

The idea of using low-end computer graphics to produce, cheaply, a huge number of shots, had actually been suggested and implemented by Knoll for the *Special Edition* films. "While we were working on *Special Edition*," Rick McCallum recalled, "John Knoll came to me and showed me a little sketch he had done. He said, 'You know, if we could buy a couple of thousand dollars' worth of gear, I think I could do all of these new space shots using this technique.' Almost every space shot we redid for *Star Wars Special Edition* was done that way. Suddenly, we had all of these wonderful shots for only two thousand bucks! So we did the same

thing for Episode I, and it worked great. If it hadn't been for these low-resolution models, the picture would have cost an extra five million dollars."

As prominent as the computer-generated work would be in Episode I—by far the biggest CG show ever—practical models and miniatures still played a crucial role, providing many shots of spaceships and extending full-size sets. "For each effect," John Knoll explained, "we used the technique that was most appropriate and best suited to the particular situation. Certain effects were easier to achieve in one medium or the other—CG or models—and we went with the medium that made the most sense. We have found that models remain the best solution to some of our effects challenges."

"Digital technology is wonderful," Rick McCallum added, "and it can do so much; but sometimes a model is still the coolest way to go." Once the effects supervisors had deter-

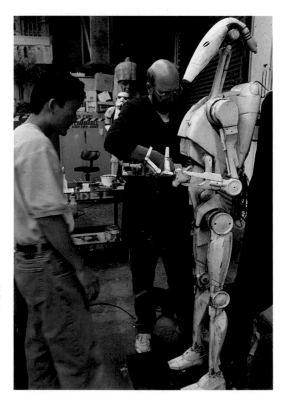

mined which shots could be done with practical models, the list was turned over to model supervisor Steve Gawley—a *Star Wars* veteran—visual effects producer Jeff Olson, and the eighty-seven-member model-shop crew, which included fellow *Star Wars* alum Lorne Peterson.

Olson was on set at Leavesden during the shoot, gathering information that would allow the model crew to extend the full-size sets through model photography. "For example," Olson explained, "only the steps and the floor of the Theed palace had been built at Leavesden for a particular scene—the rest of the set was going to be a miniature. We took precise measurements on the set to determine what we would have to build and photograph practically."

Among the other sets that would be extended through miniatures was the Mos Espa arena, only a section of which had been built on location in Tunisia. After analyzing the shots required for the sequence, Gawley and his team determined that multiple arena models in varying scales would have to be built. "You can only get so close to a miniature before you start to lose the scale," Gawley explained. "So we'd build a particular section in a larger scale, specifically for close-ups. We did that with several areas of the Podracer hangar, as well as sections of the arena."

Colored Q-Tips were positioned and photographed on a miniature stadium set to provide for background spectators in some of the Podrace shots.

Top left: John Knoll, George Lucas, Rick McCallum, and Doug Chiang visit the ILM model shop.
Top right: Visual effects supervisor Dennis Muren and model supervisor Steve Gawley inspect an MTT model.
Above right: Miniature sets were built at a variety of scales.
Above: Lucas sets up a miniature effects shot, as documentary filmmaker Jon Shenk captures the moment.

The stadium would also feature crowds of spectators. Although CG crowds would be incorporated into final shots, cloned from extras shot in the arena set in Tunisia, some practical spectators were also needed. "We needed a crowd that was three-dimensional, so that we could shoot it from a number of angles. We watched football games and car races on TV to see what huge crowds of people actually look like—and we found that it is a lot of color, but not much movement. One of the model makers came up with the idea of using Q-Tips for the spectators in some stadium shots. We colored them and

blew air at them from the back to make them sway a bit, creating the illusion that the crowd was moving." To take advantage of natural lighting, the arena models were shot outdoors, in the ILM parking lot. In other cases, the miniatures were shot in a smoke-filled stage to create the illusion of atmosphere.

In addition to the set-extension miniatures, the model shop built scaled practical models for every ship, tank, and vehicle featured in the movie—Naboo starfighters, the Queen's ship, battleships, AATs, and MTTs. Many of these models would never actually see screen time. Some were built merely as scanning models to give the CG modeling team a head start in creating the computer versions; others were built specifically as pyro models, used to capture shots of exploding spacecraft. Some, however, were detailed, painted, and filmed via motion control for compositing into otherwise computer-generated space scenes. *Motion control* refers to model photography in which a special camera is employed. A motion control camera is one that can be programmed to repeat moves far more precisely than a human camera operator could do. Essentially invented for the first *Star Wars*, motion control enables the effects team to shoot the same model multiple times, building up separate passes—such as a beauty pass, a light pass, a matte pass—which can be combined and manipulated in the final composite.

The work coming out of both the CG and the model departments would be applied to the sequences being created by all three effects units. The first of the three to start work on Episode I was Knoll's group. Upon his return from the shoot in England, Italy, and Tunisia, Knoll—with visual effects pro-

ducer Judith Weaver—began working on his slate of shots, which included street scenes in Mos Espa, the Podrace, and the space battle at the film's climax.

ILM's execution of the Podrace had actually started before principal photography, as

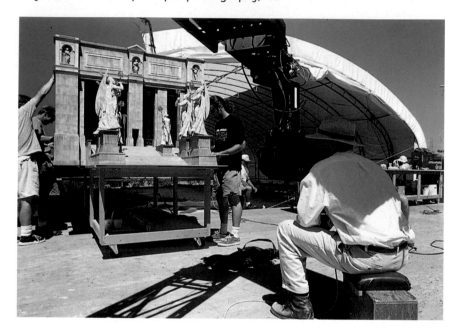

The model photography for the Podrace was conducted both on-stage and outdoors, where the crew could take advantage of natural sunlight.

Opposite page, top: Motion control cameras programmed to repeat precise moves were used to film models and miniature sets, like this one at Theed palace.
Bottom: The final Podrace sequence featured a combination of practical and CG Podracers, digital matte paintings and live-action plate photography.

soon as the sequence was locked in animatic form. The original plan had been to composite CG Podracers and characters into live aerial background plates, shot by a documentary cameraman. "But then John came to me one day, and said, 'Look—I think there is a way we can create the whole environment in CG and make it look real,'" Rick McCallum recalled. "He came up with a development budget for that, which equaled what it was going to cost to send a cameraman out to

get these aerial plates. Then John did a test for me, I showed it to George, and George said, 'Go for it.' John and his people created all of the backgrounds you see in the Podrace, the canyons and caves and everything, entirely in computer graphics."

In the end, however, the Podrace was not an all-CG sequence. As the sequence was analyzed, it became clear to Knoll that a certain percentage of shots could be achieved more efficiently with practical Podracer mod-

119

els, incorporated with CG Podracers, digital matte paintings and live-action shots of Jake Lloyd sitting at the controls of a full-size Podracer mock-up. "Some of the Podracers were still done with CG," Judith Weaver said, "but we found that, frequently, it was much more efficient and even better visually if we built a practical model, filmed it on a stage, and placed it into a shot. It was just a matter of figuring out which tool worked best for each particular shot."

Matte paintings provided the environments into which those practical models and CG elements would be placed. Matte paintings would also be used to extend many of the sets in the film, providing vast hangar interiors, for example, or vistas reaching out to the horizon. ILM artists Yusei Uesugi, Ronn Brown, Brian Flora, and Paul Huston were responsible for creating these matte paintings. Huston had worked on the original *Star Wars*, as a model maker and storyboard artist. In the ensuing years, he had become one of ILM's leading matte painters, easily making the transition from brush and canvas paintings to those created digitally. "When we did *Star Wars*," Huston recalled, "I remember George saying that someday we would be able to fly right through a matte painting; and now, thanks to digital technology, that prediction has come true. Twenty years ago, it was very difficult to move anything within a matte painting. Today, everything is possible."

For Episode I, Huston created painted backgrounds and terrain featured in the Podrace, using the animatics of the sequence for reference. "I kept the basic layout and geometry that were in the animatics," Huston said, "and created my own environment based on that. A piece of plywood with dirt on it was photographed, and that photo was used to create a texture map for the ground plane. I used other photographs as starting points, as well, manipulating them and incorporating them into the terrain and backgrounds. I constantly referred to the footage that was shot on location to match the color of the sky, the contrast, and the desert sand."

Spectators watch the Podrace from Mos Espa Arena—only a small portion of which had been built and shot on location. It was the effects team's job to take the location footage and expand it, simulating a giant stadium filled with thousands of alien and human spectators. A total of 350,000 characters were added to the sequence, most of which were tiny CG specks in the far background of the stadium. For more foreground characters, Knoll shot extras dressed in Tatooine garb and wearing foam latex masks. That footage was then translated into digital form, where it could be tweaked and cloned until the size of the crowd had reached the hundreds of thousands.

One of the interesting aspects of shooting the extras for the stadium crowd scenes was that Knoll used high-definition digital video, rather than film stock. Digital video was used to shoot a variety of elements, including the occasional live-action, as a test to see if it would hold up when it was intercut with normal film stock. It did, convincing Lucas to shoot Episodes II and III entirely on digital videotape.

For the Mos Espa street scenes, Knoll's team had to add computer-generated characters into live-action elements shot on the set in Tunisia. But the assignment wasn't just a matter of arbitrarily adding CG characters. Rather, each character had to be given its own through-line of action. "If we put a CG character in a shot," Judith Weaver explained, "we had to have it *doing* something. We had to come up with a story for

Live-action shots of Mos Espa were supplemented with model photography of the town, built in miniature by the ILM model crew.

that character. We couldn't just stick things in the background. There had to be a reason for it to be there."

In addition to populating the streets of Mos Espa with CG characters, the team extended the live-action set considerably. "We built some miniatures for the extension of Mos Espa in the background," Knoll explained. "We took pictures of those miniatures in the parking lot at ILM, scanned them into a computer, and blended that imagery with additional painted buildings and all the other elements. So, in just one shot, we had a lot of different techniques involved."

Foreground characters would also be created for the Mos Espa sequence—most notably, Watto the junk dealer. Watto, in fact, was the first CG character tackled by Knoll and his team. "Watto was a very complicated character," Knoll commented. "He had a lot of details that we had to animate—his wings, which were constantly in motion, his feet, his clothing, even a little cord attached to his tool belt. We had to write a computer program just for that cord, in fact." As the first garbed CG character attempted for the show, Watto was a testing

ground for the cloth simulation that had been developed by the software team during the research and development phase at ILM. "We learned a lot from Watto. Creating his leather vest is what helped us get Jar Jar's clothing done. We also used the same simulation program developed for the cord on Watto's tool belt for the flapping of Jar Jar's ears."

The space battle between Naboo and Trade Federation starfighters and the penetration of the Neimoidian battleship near the end of the film were as dynamic and complex as the Podrace sequence. Like most of the major effects sequences, the space battle was realized through a combination of computer animation and motion-control model photography. Practical models were filmed on the motion-control stages at ILM. Since all the camera moves had been worked out in the animatics already approved by Lucas, in many cases the motion data in those animatics was downloaded directly into the motion-control camera. While the computer assist enabled the photography crews to generally replicate the camera moves in the animatics, that replication was not precise— primarily because the parameters of the vir-

121

tual camera and those of the real motion-control camera were not identical. However, the technique usually managed to get the shot 90 percent of the way there; and adjustments and tweaks could be performed after the fact to make the shot more closely resemble its counterpart in the animatic.

High-resolution 3-D computer models were also built for hero shots—featured shots in which the ships would be in the foreground or in relative close-up—while a large number of background spaceships were created in low-resolution 2-D. Many of the ships were produced in all three forms: practical model, 3-D model, and lower-resolution model, each of which would be used as needed for specific shots. The Queen's ship, for example, was built as a ten-foot miniature for close-ups of the craft stranded in the desert of Tatooine. A 3-D version of the ship was computer generated for shots requiring complex animation. And the low-res computer model was employed for quick cuts of the ship in space.

In addition to the Mos Espa, Podrace, and space battle shots, Knoll's unit was responsible for digitally removing the pup-peteer operating C-3PO in each and every one of the character's shots. It was less visible, less glamorous work than the races and battles; but it was a crucial task that enabled Lucas to realize an entirely skeletal C-3PO—a design that could not have been accommodated by a performer in a suit. Replacing the human figure behind the C-3PO puppet with the appropriate areas from a clean plate took months of painstaking work.

Dennis Muren's group, which would produce shots for the underwater and ground battle sequences, started with the underwater scenes. Among the shots required for the

Models of the Queen's ship and the Naboo starfighter were built at a variety of scales to accommodate the needs of specific shots.

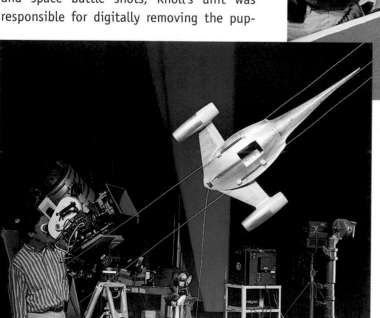

Above: Every live-action shot of an ambulatory C-3PO included, by necessity, the figure of the puppeteer behind him. In postproduction, ILM went through the methodical and time-consuming process of digitally "painting out" the operator frame by frame. Right: A major force in the making of the original *Star Wars* trilogy, Dennis Muren—one of three visual effects supervisors on *The Phantom Menace*—came full circle career-wise with Episode I.

sequence were underwater canyons and cliffs and tunnels—the terrain through which Obi-Wan would navigate the submarine after their departure from the underwater city of Otoh Gunga. Since the submarine and the city itself—in fact, the majority of the sequence—would be computer generated, Muren had considered realizing the underwater terrain through CG, as well. That notion was quickly cast aside, in favor of creating terrain models and shooting them in a

smoke-filled room to simulate the murky, watery depths. "I felt my CG team should be busy doing the things that *only* CG can do," Muren offered. "This work I knew could be done practically, using models." Spiky cliffs, canyons, tunnels, and caves were built in small scale, carved out of dense foam, and painted. These models were then set up on one of ILM's stages, where a motion control camera filmed them through layers of dense smoke.

Those model photography backgrounds were ultimately combined with computer-generated elements such as the submarine and three sea monsters—the opee sea killer, the colo claw fish, and the sando aqua monster. While working principally from the art department's sea monster concept designs, the CG team sought additional guidance by observing real fish and other animals. A computer model was made for each of the creatures, which was then animated and, finally, rendered out. In the case of the colo claw fish, rendering included shaders—software tools that apply specific textures to CG models—to make the fish look as if it were glowing. "To make sure the audience could distinguish one sea monster from the other," visual effects producer Ned Gorman explained, "we gave each creature its own

city was a combination of a miniature set, a partially built full-size set, computer-generated characters, and bluescreen elements of Qui-Gon and Obi-Wan. "We were a little concerned as to how that would all come together," Ned Gorman admitted. "But looking at the scene once it was done, it was just remarkable. You accept everything, and it is completely believable. You are completely sucked into this Otoh Gunga world personality and characteristics." The creatures were finally composited with the model backgrounds, which were enhanced digitally to make the smoke elements read more clearly as an underwater environment.

The establishing shot of the city of Otoh Gunga was *entirely* computer generated; however, a scene within a boardroom in the

Top left: Working closely with Muren was visual effects producer Ned Gorman.
Above and left: One of the major sequences created by the Muren/Gorman team was the underwater chase. Underwater terrain was carved out of foam, painted, then shot on a smoke-filled stage to simulate the underwater environment.

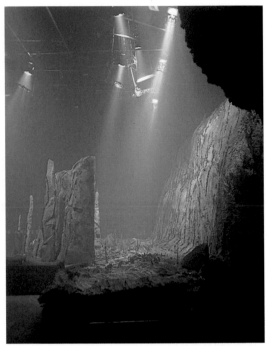

The model photography elements were combined with a computer-generated submarine and various creatures for the scene in which Obi-Wan, Qui-Gon, and Jar Jar encounter a series of sea monsters.

because it is so compelling and real."

Muren and his crew were also responsible for shots leading up to the underwater sequence—a swamp scene in which Qui-Gon first meets Jar Jar Binks. In the story, the Trade Federation invasion of Naboo is announced with the arrival of hovering tanks, which dispatch the droid army. The tanks' appearance near the swamp initiates a

stampede of *Star Wars*–style animals. Live-action elements of Liam Neeson, shot in front of a bluescreen, were integrated with computer-generated images of the stampeding animals, tanks, and backgrounds. Muren had supervised a similar CG stampede

for *The Lost World* a couple of years earlier; but in Episode I, both stampeding animals *and* the terrain upon which they run would have to be computer generated. "In *The Lost World*," Ned Gorman, who had acted as visual effects producer on that film, recalled, "we put our CG dinosaurs into live-action background plates shot on location. For Episode I, we had to create both the background and the creatures." Those backgrounds, consisting of ground, grass, and trees, were generated for the entire thirty-second stampede sequence.

The Muren team's other major sequence, the huge ground battle on Naboo near the end of the film, was saved for the second half of the effects schedule, and was far more difficult than the underwater scenes. "The land battle was a bigger challenge," Muren explained, "because it took place in broad daylight. Daylight scenes require much more attention to detail, and everything has to look exactly right. But I liked that aspect of it. I think if you're going to do a battle of

the dimension of this one, you should be able to see it."

Backgrounds for the entirely synthetic sequence were assembled from still photographs of green hills and valleys, shot by Dennis Muren. Those photographs were scanned into the computers at ILM, then distorted slightly to make them look less like an Earth terrain, and more like something that would be found on the alien planet of Naboo. CG images of tanks, droids, and the Gungan army were then inserted into those backgrounds. The entire epic-scale battle had been choreographed in animatics previously—although Muren revised those animatics somewhat when he took on the sequence.

For the droid and Gungan armies, ILM had to computer-generate believable, dynamic performances. "The challenge, always," Muren said, "is to bring a performance out of those digital characters. For instance, George came up with this great idea of having the droids react like pigeons.

A finalized shot of the opee sea killer as it latches onto the Gungan submarine. Working principally from the art department's sea monster concepts, the CG team found additional guidance by observing real fish and other marine life.

They kind of flock together, and they're not too smart—which eventually causes their downfall." The Gungans featured in the battle would display a far more organic and random style of behavior. Other living creatures featured in the sequence are the kaadu and fambaas that the Gungans ride into battle. Animators were sent on horse-riding expeditions to get a feel for the animals' shifting weight and mass, as well as to determine how the Gungan riders would move astride the creatures.

The battle would also feature hundreds of effects such as explosions, laser fire, and the glowing "energy balls" and protective shield used by the Gungan army. Practical explosions were shot onstage, then composited into the sequence on ILM's Sabre digital

Each of the three sea monsters in this sequence were endowed with specific behaviors and physical characteristics to ensure audiences would be able to distinguish one from another.
Right: The sando aqua monster.
Below: The colo claw fish.

compositing system. "We also used some stock footage of explosions," Ned Gorman said. "The Sabre team scanned all the explosion elements into the system, then positioned, distorted, and manipulated them as each shot required."

Intended for the compositing of relatively low-resolution elements, the Sabre cannot be used for every shot; but it is an extremely fast system for those occasions

This page and next: One of the most challenging aspects of the computer animation assignment was animating a mass of characters, such as the thousands of droids featured in the ground battle at the film's end. Walking, running, battling, and other action cycles were developed, then randomly assigned to individual characters by the computer.

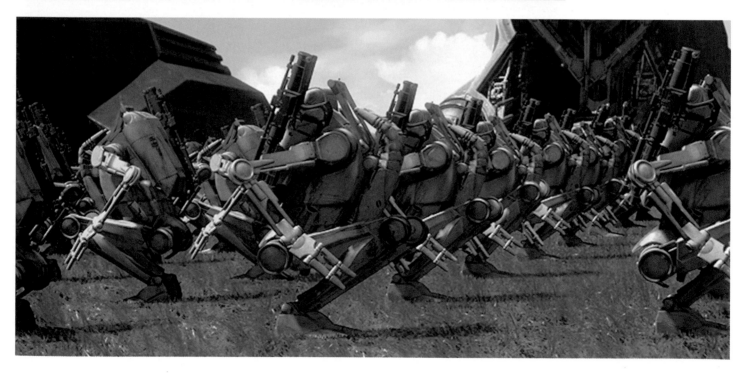

when a low-res image will suffice. "We can start with a background created by the digital matte department, for instance," Sabre supervisor Pablo Helman explained, "and add elements, shadows, camera shakes. The system is also very interactive. Dennis Muren could sit right there with Sabre artist Chad Taylor, ask for a changed element or any kind

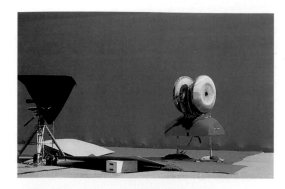

shield was a color with some digital noise and an electrical pattern added to it. I placed it over the backgrounds and distorted it. Dennis was at my side as I played with it; and thanks to Sabre technology, we were able to experiment with a wide range of things and get instant results."

Scott Squires's team worked simultaneously with the other two units and was responsible for creating the movie's hologram and lightsaber effects. The holograms, in particular, would be far more sophisticated than they had been in the original trilogy. To realize the effect, the second unit crew in England filmed actors against black- or blue-screen. At ILM, that footage was put through special filters that added noise, simulating a video image.

Although new technology would also be used for the lightsaber effects, for the sake of continuity such effects had to replicate those in the first three films. "The technique we're using is a bit more sophisticated,"

of variation—and he could see that change immediately."

The Sabre was also useful in creating the shield and energy ball effects. Though the energy balls were basically variations on the glowing wand lightsaber effect, the protective energy shield required a lot of finessing before an appropriate look was achieved. In Sabre, Chad Taylor created several versions of the shield's surface to show to Muren. "Some of them had small waves rippling over the surface," Taylor said, "others had big waves. We tried a variety of colors. Essentially, the

Far left: For the ground battle, the model shop produced models of tanks and, pictured here, the Gungan shield generator. The models were rigged with pyrotechnics to explode on cue, and that footage was subsequently composited into ground battle shots. Left: Scott Squires was the third visual effects supervisor and was responsible for views of the city of Theed, as well as lightsaber and energy beam effects.

Maul, Obi-Wan, and Qui-Gon engage in a long lightsaber battle. In addition to the lightsabers, the scene featured pulsating energy beams crisscrossing the expanse of the corridor. "A very small portion of the generator room was built in England," Squires explained, "and from that, we created a huge room measuring six hundred feet across, as well as a huge pit—all through CG. The electrical beams were also computer generated. We blended the virtual set with the set built on the soundstage."

Bluescreen areas had been set up on stage to facilitate the matting in of the set extensions and energy beams. The actors and the practical areas of the set also had to be lit in such a way to suggest the interactive lighting coming from the pulsating beams. "When we shot the scene," director of photography David Tattersall explained, "we didn't

Above: Visual effects producer Heather Smith.
Below: Live-action scenes featuring lightsabers were scanned digitally so the CG glowing effect could be integrated into the footage frame by frame.

Squires said, "but it is still faithful to the look that was created in the previous films." Where, originally, the lightsabers were done using a photochemical process, with different layers of film being processed together optically, for Episode I the lightsaber scenes were scanned digitally, and the glowing sabre effect was painted in frame by frame. The scene was then recorded back out to film.

Lightsaber effects would dominate the scene in the generator complex, where Darth

know yet how big the beams would end up being, or what color they would be. Eventually we came up with a purplish color, which was reflected on the actors and on all the practical parts of the set." Later on, energy beams of the same color replaced the bluescreen areas. On-set strobes and flashing lights heightened the illusion of interactivity between the digital energy-beam effect and the live-action footage.

These energy "gates" lock in on the Jedi in the course of their fight with Darth Maul, another effect created in the Sabre. "We developed the look of the energy doors," Pablo Helman explained, "going from some of the concept art. We then used the Sabre to design the energy doors and work out how they should open and close, the noise pattern, how much they should glow and the kind of energy that should emanate from them."

Squires's team also contributed shots to the council chamber sequence inside the Jedi Temple, adding to the circular set built

The final lightsaber battle in the generator complex was shot on a minimal set surrounded by bluescreen to facilitate the matting in of digital set extensions. Opposite page: Squires's unit created holograms that were far more sophisticated than those featured in the original trilogy. Here, Governor Sio Bibble speaks to Queen Amidala aboard her starship, via hologram.

at Leavesden a variety of matte paintings to reveal the views outside the temple windows. "We did three different sets of matte paintings," visual effects producer Heather Smith said. "One set for daytime, another for sunset, and another for nighttime. It was an interesting exercise to take the same backgrounds and adjust them for three different times of day." The team also had to digitally adjust the lighting inside the room itself, matching the time of day as it was revealed through the windows.

For the Galactic Senate sequence, Squires's unit added flying computer-generated boxes or platforms, upon which various characters—both live-action and CG—stand. "Portions of the main tower, two boxes, and a bit of the wall were built on the set in England," Squires revealed, "but there had to be thousands of these flying boxes in the scene. So we added those, as well as the computer-generated characters standing in the boxes." Finally, Squires and his crew provided shots for the end parade, which featured extensive CG and model work. CG confetti was added, matched to the practical confetti used in the live-action plates. The lighting in those plates—shot in broad daylight—was also changed to suggest a golden-hour dusk scene.

Each unit reviewed its own shots independently on a daily basis, while all of the groups joined to watch the three units' dailies at least once a week. Tuesday mornings would usually find George Lucas seated in ILM's screening room, reviewing and com-

menting on the progress of that week's shots. "In order to make our deadline," Chrissie England commented, "we had to final thirty-five shots a week. It was a race to the finish."

"The only reason we were able to realize so much," John Knoll added, "was because of George. He had a very specific vision, and he had no trouble articulating that vision to the different units. He always said that he only directed half of the movie during principal photography; the rest he directed afterward, here at ILM."

The artists and technicians at ILM continued to work on shots clear up until their April 23, 1997, deadline. Despite the huge number of effects, and the inevitable time crunch as that date neared, both Lucas and those at ILM remained confident that the work would meet their own expectations and those of the *Star Wars* fans. It was a confidence they had not been able to enjoy the first time around. "When I started the first

Star Wars," Lucas recalled, "everybody said it was impossible. I even recall telling the effects team, back in 1977, 'At this point in time, this is impossible. We can't do it.' But I went on faith and did it anyway, not knowing what the results would be. This time, even though I pushed ILM into frontiers

Above: Scenes inside the Jedi Temple were shot on a circular set in front of blue-screens that would later be replaced with matte painted views of Coruscant.
Below: Editor Paul Martin Smith.

134

The view through the temple windows would reveal daylight, sunset, or nighttime, depending on the scene. Lighting was adjusted accordingly, both on the live-action set and on the digital matte paintings inserted into the window areas.

they'd never been to before, I knew, based on my twenty-year-long relationship with the company, that they could do it, and that they'd come through."

Just as the visual effects effort spanned the duration of the preproduction, production, and postproduction periods, the editing of Episode I was an ongoing process that

extended from the time shooting started in England to just weeks before the film's release. Editor Paul Martin Smith, another veteran of *The Young Indiana Jones Chronicles*, was in England throughout production, working with an English crew of assistants. Once he returned to Skywalker Ranch, at the end of the shoot, Smith would work with Ben Burtt and George Lucas, continuing to edit—and reedit—the movie over the course of the next two years. "It was a very small editing unit," McCallum said. "And that allowed us to edit for two years for the same amount of money it takes to edit a typical film in six months." Smith focused on editing the dramatic, dialogue-heavy scenes, while Burtt—who had been instrumental in developing the animatics during preproduction—concentrated on action sequences.

The editing process was, in George Lucas's mind, the most important phase of making the movie. "I came out of editing and I've worked as an editor," Lucas said, "so my whole focus on filmmaking is as an edi-

Padmé becomes," Lucas explained. "When I was writing the script, I didn't realize how strong she would be as a character in her own right—mainly because, in my mind, I didn't really separate her from the Queen. But when I saw the movie cut together I realized that the audience gets very attached to her, then she disappears, and then she reappears at the end, almost as an after-thought. I thought I should explain what happens to her somehow—and this scene with Anakin was a way to do that."

Another added scene, shot after princi-pal photography had wrapped, was one in which Palpatine congratulates the Queen on her victory, and the Neimoidians, Nute and Rune, are sent to the Galactic Senate. "In the original script," Lucas said, "Nute and Rune were packed off in a scene with the Queen in the throne room. But I discovered, after the screening, that I really needed a scene with Palpatine coming back to estab-lish that he was now the Supreme Chancellor. I also needed Palpatine to acknowledge the character of Anakin in some way. So I took

all of those story points and blended them into one new scene."

The first of the pickup scenes was filmed at Leavesden in August 1998; three more pickup periods would be scheduled through-out the following seven months. These short filming periods were easily accommodated, due to the fact that requisite sets were still intact at Leavesden. "It was never difficult to keep all the sets in place for the pickups

The language spoken by Jar Jar and other Gungan char-acters was a mixture of bro-ken English and nonsense words, interpreted by the vocal performers, then enhanced slightly by sound designer Ben Burtt.

For many characters on Tatooine, Burtt re-created 'Huttese', a language he had developed for the original trilogy.
Above: Jabba the Hutt salutes the crowd with a greeting in Huttese at the Mos Espa Arena.
Right: Sound designer Ben Burtt.

because we'd always planned it that way," Rick McCallum explained.

Even as pickup shots were being filmed in England, and the visual effects and editing teams were executing their duties, another full-scale effort was on-going at Skywalker Sound, situated on the grounds of Skywalker Ranch—the mixing and recording of sound effects for Episode I. The original *Star Wars* trilogy had been as much a sound extravaganza as a visual spectacle; and years of work and experimentation had gone into creating R2-D2's beeps and whistles, the electronic hum of the lightsabers, the alien languages, and all the other sounds of *Star Wars*.

Ben Burtt, who had been instrumental in creating those sounds, returned to the *Star Wars* trilogy as Episode I's sound designer. Roughly one thousand new sound effects had to be created for the movie, produced at a rate of ten to twelve per day. After watching a rough cut of the film, Burtt organized the sound effects into categories, then began producing them by experimenting and

manipulating sounds on a Synclavier—an instrument similar to a synthesizer. "Instead of having music on the keys," Burtt explained, "I have sounds. And I can perform and play those sounds as if I was composing music. I also have a large library of sounds that I can sample on the keyboard. The sound effects are designed through trial and error, and a lot of listening."

The language of the Neimoidians was based on recordings of foreign-born people speaking English.
Top: The Neimoidian Viceroy Nute Gunray at Theed Palace.
Middle and bottom: Nute Gunray, Rune Haako, and Daultay Dofine are confronted by the Sith Lord Darth Sidious via hologram.

Creating voices is one of the most difficult aspects of the sound design task, whether those voices are speaking an alien language or English with a special sound treatment. "When you invent the sound of a new vehicle," Burtt said, "people have nothing to compare it to in real life, so they tend to accept the sound, whatever it is. But the opposite is true of voices. There has to be a ring of truth there, otherwise the audience won't believe it."

Among Episode I's English-speaking aliens are the Neimoidians and the Gungans. The former's language was made up of foreign-born people speaking English. "We tried to find dialects that were not recognizable," Burtt said, "or at least not strongly associated with a specific culture." Gunganese was made up of both English words and nonsense words; the Gungans would invert phrases, creating the impression of a subculture living on the planet of Naboo.

"Creating a language for a creature like Jar Jar was a way of developing characters as well as an ambiance," George Lucas said. "It was something we needed to do in a film like Episode I. To me, it always seems phony when characters in science fiction movies speak English perfectly, with no accent. That's not the way the world is."

The language Lucas devised for Jar Jar was understandable—but only up to a point. "You understand half of it," Ben Burtt explained, "and the rest you have to figure out. Ahmed Best had a huge input into the design of the language because of the way he performed the character. His vocal abilities brought tremendous originality to the language." Best was so close to what Lucas wanted in Jar Jar's vocal performance, the actor's audio remained pretty much intact for the final film, except for a minimum of technical processing.

The non-English-speaking characters included some that were making a return appearance in the world of *Star Wars*. Jabba the Hutt, for example, would speak the Huttese language first introduced by Greedo in *Star Wars*. "Huttese was inspired by an Incan language called Catua," Burtt said. "I heard a language tape once of someone speaking in Catua, and I liked the sound of it. We took the sound and even some of the words of that language, and wrote them down phonetically. Out of that came Huttese."

For C-3PO, Burtt processed Anthony Daniels's voice electronically, then added an echo. Burtt vocalized some of R2-D2's sounds himself and mixed them with elements from a synthesizer. Here, C-3PO and R2-D2 are seen in the Podrace hangar.

The hum of the lightsabers was created by combining the motor sound of an old movie projector and the buzz from a television set with electronic processing. Left: Obi-Wan Kenobi and Darth Maul battle in the Theed generator complex.

An entire sense of character for R2-D2 had been communicated with the little droid's now-familiar vocalizations—and would again in Episode I. "What was discovered through trial and error," Burtt said, "was that babies make sounds that we as parents understand. They can sound happy, sad, or angry, all communicated through whimpers, high-pitched sounds, sighs, et cetera. So at the time, we thought maybe we could do the same thing with Artoo." Burtt himself vocalized some of the sounds, then mixed them with elements from a synthesizer to give them a mechanical, electronic quality.

Although Anthony Daniels provided the voice for C-3PO, Burtt did a little electronic processing on Daniels's voice to take out some of the low frequencies. "We also did some 'phasing,'" Burtt explained, "which is when you add a short echo to the voice to give it a ringing quality. In this film,

Threepio had to sound a bit different because of his different appearance—but the voice was still familiar." For the battle droids, Burtt took the voice of a highway patrolman and made it sound as if it was being transmitted from a speaker.

The sound for the lightsabers would be updated slightly, but still retain the quality of the original. The hum of the lightsaber had been realized originally by combining the motor of an old movie projector and a buzz that Burtt had recorded by accident when a microphone got too close to a television set. A signal went through the microphone, causing the audible buzzing sound. For Darth Maul's double-sided lightsaber, Burtt re-created the original sound, then added a ripple to break up the constant tone.

A similar approach was taken for the roar of the spaceship engines. Burtt listened for a sound that was reminiscent of the original, but with a new twist. "I tried to come

The sounds of the Podracers were designed to enhance the excitement of a high speed, high risk competition.
Far right: Podrace champion Sebulba.
Below: The Podrace approaches an explosive finale.
High-speed car races of the fifties and sixties inspired the souped-up engine sounds for the Podrace.

up with sounds that seemed natural," Burtt said. "Most spaceship sounds are akin to World War II propeller aircraft noises that have been altered and slowed down. There is a pulse to them, rather than a continuous hum. If I was dealing with a ship that related to a specific character, I tried to match the sound of that ship to the spirit of that character. For the Queen's ship, for instance, the sound was both powerful and smooth, because the ship was shiny and elegant. By comparison, the *Millennium Falcon* in the

first trilogy was very powerful, but also like a hot rod—so it rattled and sounded as if it were homemade. The TIE fighters were supposed to be very frightening, so they screamed at you as they flew by."

The Podrace was inspired by high-speed car races of the fifties and sixties; and the director wanted the sound of the racing Pods to mirror that, with high-pitched, screaming engines and the sound of gears shifting. "It's

Left: The Gungan submarine explores the murky depths of Naboo's core. Muted, subtle sounds for the submarine engine were created through an electronic musical effect combined with the sound of small motors. Below left: Vocalization from marine life and land mammals were blended for the deep-pitched sounds that emanate from the sea monsters.

a challenging sequence because it is very fast, with a lot of cuts," Burtt said. "Every time there was a new image, I needed to add a new sound. Sound is always relative to the number of cuts in the movie. The sound has to evolve, go up and down. It's got to be exciting."

Some of the excitement of the Podrace would be stimulated by the sounds of the spectators watching from Mos Espa Arena. Burtt took a recorder to a San Francisco 49ers football game and recorded the crowd's audible reactions. "We couldn't have hired

that many people, brought them to a studio, and recorded them. I got three hours of different levels of crowd reactions, and I input them on a keyboard so I could play them on the synthesizer."

The underwater sequence, in contrast to the Podrace, required sounds that were muted and subtle. "Dennis Muren had to make the sequence *look* murky and dark," Burtt said, "and I had to make it sound the same way, through sound effects that were muted and muffled." Burtt divided the sound requirements into two basic categories—submarine and sea monster. The sub sounds were an electronic musical effect, combined with the sound of small motors. For the sea monsters, Burtt started with recordings he had made of whales; but Lucas felt that the sound was too high-pitched. "He wanted a deeper sound for the monsters, something like what you would hear from a dinosaur. I ended up blending marine-life sounds and land-based mammal sounds for the monsters."

Layers and layers of sound were required for complex sequences such as the stampede and the ground battle. In the stampede, for example, many things happen at once: giant

Trade Federation transport ships approach the planet; tanks are dispatched to hover over the surface; trees are mowed down as the large vehicles thunder through the forest; and hundreds of animals stampede over the terrain. In such instances, dramatic license is called for—because, in reality, such an event would create a cacophonous roar, with one sound indistinguishable from another. "I had to layer the sounds in very carefully for the stampede," Burtt said. "I took all the sounds of the tanks and Trade Federation transports and made them very low and deep. Then I started layering on top of that sounds that were different in spectral quality: I put in the animal grunts and barks

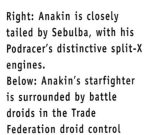

Right: Anakin is closely tailed by Sebulba, with his Podracer's distinctive split-X engines.
Below: Anakin's starfighter is surrounded by battle droids in the Trade Federation droid control ship in one of the final scenes.

as they're being chased through the forest. I used all kinds of animal sounds, from caribou to cows to bears and rhinoceroses, modifying them to sound otherworldly. Then I added the highest frequency sounds, which were the birds and flying reptiles. Finally, I put in the tree and foliage sounds, which tended to cover all frequencies."

Rather than use electronic, synthesized audio elements, Burtt decided to mix the sounds of real motors for the ships in the ground battle. "What made it hard for the sound design," Burtt explained, "was that there were so many shots cut together so quickly. The eye can pick up visual information very quickly, but sound takes longer. The quicker the shot, the shorter the time for you to identify a sound. It is very hard to design sounds within that context."

In late January 1999, sound editors Tom Bellfort and Tom Johnson began to premix the movie's sound, which included not only Ben Burtt's sound effects, but also dialogue recorded both during production and separately, in a recording studio. Still missing, however, was the music. Music is an important element of every film, but especially so in the films of George Lucas. "When I write the script," Lucas said, "I hear the movie more in terms of music than I do in terms of sound effects. I can actually hear it in my mind. I pay a lot of attention to the music, even during the early stages of writing. The *Star Wars* movies are, in essence, silent movies because they are stories that are told visually; and in silent movies the relationship between image and music is everything. A lot of the story and a lot of the emotion

Droid army commander OOM-9 surveys the battle-ground on the surface of Naboo.

are told through the music. It is one of the most important elements of a film."

John Williams would compose the musical score for Episode I, just as he had done for all three original *Star Wars* movies, the *Indiana Jones* trilogy, *Jaws, E.T.: The Extra-Terrestrial, Schindler's List*, and fifty-nine other films. His movie scores have earned the composer five Academy Awards and an incredible thirty-six Oscar nominations, and they contain some of the most recognizable musical themes in movie history.

The first week in February 1999, John Williams, George Lucas, and Rick McCallum returned to England for the scoring of the film—but Williams had been on the show for several months by that time. "I first saw a cut of Episode I at the beginning of October 1998," Williams recalled. "It was a bit raw and all the special effects weren't in yet, but all the timings were there. I was anxious to get started as soon as I could. We had to record the music in February, so, at that point, I had only four months to prepare a score that was two hours long."

Williams came to that first viewing of the film with the music from the first trilogy very much on his mind. "The existing music was already in my head," Williams explained,

"as were thematic identifications with certain characters or ideas in the story. The next step was to create a series of melodic motifs that were new to this film and would coexist with the old ones." The way in which the preexisting themes and motifs were blended with the new would be one of the most challenging and interesting aspects of the new film's score. In composing a music theme for the character of Anakin, for example, Williams was compelled to include a hint of the theme he had composed for Darth Vader for the original trilogy. "Anakin's theme definitely includes a series of musical clues that people might recognize as the music of someone else we've already encountered."

New musical themes included those for the characters of Jar Jar and Qui-Gon. "Jar Jar's theme was comical, because that is his function in the story. But Qui-Gon's theme had to do with nobility, because he is a teacher, a master, a moral conscience for the young Jedi. There was also a new evil march for the Trade Federation army, which wasn't at all like the music of Darth Vader from the previous films, even though it has the same function. It creates the same kind of weight and has great force behind it."

After seeing the film for the first time,

Williams spent two days rewatching it with Lucas at his side. "We call it a 'spotting session,'" Williams explained. "We watched the film without the temp track and decided where we would start and stop the music. George explained what the dramatic function of the music would be, scene by scene. A spotting session is a starting point for a director, a composer, and a sound designer to begin to realize where we're going to be soft or loud, where we're going to accelerate or slow down. It is a general discussion about how the music will ride along with the sound effects and the dialogue. At the end of that session, I went away; and four months later, I came back with two hours of orchestral music to accompany the film."

Lucas would not hear that music until the actual scoring sessions at the end of January. "Some directors, like Steven Spielberg, for example, like to come in as you are composing and hear ideas," Williams explained. "But George didn't do that. For one thing, he was in San Francisco and I was in Los Angeles. Another reason was that a film like this one is a colossal job of musical design—and I write every note myself, without a team of people with me. When you ask an architect to build a giant building—espe-

cially in only four months—you'd better go away, leave him alone, let him do the job, and just hope the building stands when it is finished. That's what George did."

Williams started the score in the middle of the film, composing music for scenes between Anakin and his mother. "I wanted to get to the human aspect of the story before I got into the action sequences," Williams explained. "I also wanted to base the music in the action scenes on a more human, thematic, emotional aspect." Williams then moved on to the end of the film. "It was important for me to know where I was riding to, so I could work toward that."

Williams, Lucas, McCallum, and the London Symphony Orchestra gathered at Abbey Road Studios in London, where the scoring sessions would take place over the course of eight days. Just as it was for so many *Star Wars* veterans working on the film, Episode I was like a family reunion for John Williams. "Working on this film was like coming back to an old friend," Williams said. "To me, it seemed very much like the same experience I had twenty years ago, even though the characters were different. It had a familiar connection, a thread of family unity through all of it."

John Williams conducts the London Symphony Orchestra during the scoring sessions.

Rick McCallum and George Lucas share a moment with their favorite astromech droid in Tunisia.

The final sound mix was put together and added to the movie in March, with the remaining visual effects shots delivered in April. After four years, Episode I was at last completed; and, already, George Lucas and Rick McCallum were looking toward Episode II. Lucas, in fact, had been writing the next movie in the trilogy ever since June 1998, and had known the rough outline of that story since before he'd started his work on Episode I. "I couldn't have done Episode I without knowing the complete story," Lucas remarked. "It was all mapped out, and I knew what the story was—I just had to write specific scenes. But it was still quite a challenge, because Episode II required that I write a love story in the middle of a *Star Wars* movie. Basically, that's what Episode II is—a love story, with the Sith's relentless drive to take over the universe in the background. The challenge was to balance those two things."

The art department at Skywalker Ranch would jump into designing elements for the next episode in June 1999, just a month after Episode I's release. And Rick McCallum was scheduled to leave for his first location scout *one day* after the movie's release. "Gavin Bocquet and I will go off for three months to find locations in Tunisia, Italy, Portugal, and Spain," McCallum said. In fact, McCallum already had been making trips to Australia, where Episode II would be shot, every three months or so throughout the last year of postproduction on Episode I. "I wanted another new place and another new group for the next movie. I found a huge warehouse in Australia, near the Fox Studios, and we'll build some of our sets there so we can keep them up as long as we need them."

But all of that planning and preparation was for another movie, another time. For now, for Episode I, all that remained for George Lucas, Rick McCallum, and the two thousand–plus men and women who had contributed to the production was to wait for the movie's May 21, 1999, release—and for the world's reaction. "I don't think of myself as the best writer or director in the world," Lucas concluded. "I've never equated my opinion of what I do with the rest of the world's opinion of what I do. And because of that, I am always a little amazed when I do a movie and it is so well received. But just like all the other *Star Wars* movies, for every person who loves Episode I, there will be two or three who hate it, or who won't see it and couldn't care less about the whole thing. All I can do now is throw it out there in the real world—and wait to see what everyone thinks. We'll see..."

STAR WARS EPISODE I

Opposite page: The Episode I "teaser" poster was produced in November 1998 in conjunction with the release of the first theatrical trailer in the United States.

CREDITS AS OF APRIL 1, 1999

WRITTEN & DIRECTED BY
GEORGE LUCAS

PRODUCED BY
RICK McCALLUM

EXECUTIVE PRODUCER
GEORGE LUCAS

DIRECTOR OF PHOTOGRAPHY
DAVID TATTERSALL, B.S.C.

PRODUCTION DESIGNER
GAVIN BOCQUET

EDITED BY
PAUL MARTIN SMITH G.B.F.E.
BEN BURTT

COSTUME DESIGNER
TRISHA BIGGAR

CASTING BY
ROBIN GURLAND

MUSIC BY
JOHN WILLIAMS

Starring

LIAM NEESON

EWAN McGREGOR

NATALIE PORTMAN

JAKE LLOYD   PERNILLA AUGUST

AND FRANK OZ AS YODA

Co-Starring

IAN McDIARMID   OLIVER FORD DAVIES   HUGH QUARSHIE

AHMED BEST   ANTHONY DANIELS   KENNY BAKER

WITH TERENCE STAMP
AS CHANCELLOR VALORUM

DESIGN DIRECTOR
DOUG CHIANG

VISUAL EFFECTS SUPERVISORS
JOHN KNOLL   DENNIS MUREN   SCOTT SQUIRES

ANIMATION DIRECTOR
ROB COLEMAN

PRODUCTION SUPERVISOR
DAVID BROWN

FIRST ASSISTANT DIRECTOR
CHRIS NEWMAN

SECOND ASSISTANT DIRECTOR
BERNARD BELLEW

THIRD ASSISTANT DIRECTOR
BEN HOWARTH

Cast

QUI-GON JINN	LIAM NEESON
OBI-WAN KENOBI	EWAN McGREGOR
QUEEN AMIDALA/PADMÉ	NATALIE PORTMAN
ANAKIN SKYWALKER	JAKE LLOYD
SENATOR PALPATINE	IAN McDIARMID
SHMI SKYWALKER	PERNILLA AUGUST
SIO BIBBLE	OLIVER FORD DAVIES
CAPTAIN PANAKA	HUGH QUARSHIE
JAR JAR BINKS	AHMED BEST
C-3PO	ANTHONY DANIELS
R2-D2	KENNY BAKER
YODA	FRANK OZ
CHANCELLOR VALORUM	TERENCE STAMP
BOSS NASS	BRIAN BLESSED
WATTO	ANDREW SECOMBE
DARTH MAUL	RAY PARK
SEBULBA	LEWIS MACLEOD
WALD	WARWICK DAVIS
CAPTAIN TARPALS	STEVEN SPEIRS
NUTE GUNRAY	SILAS CARSON
RUNE HAAKO	JEROME BLAKE
DAULTAY DOFINE	ALAN RUSCOE
RIC OLIÉ	RALPH BROWN
FIGHTER PILOT BRAVO 5	CELIA IMRIE
FIGHTER PILOT BRAVO 2	BENEDICT TAYLOR
FIGHTER PILOT BRAVO 3	CLARENCE SMITH
MACE WINDU	SAMUEL L. JACKSON

PALACE GUARD	DOMINIC WEST
RABÉ	CRISTINA da SILVA
EIRTAÉ	FRIDAY (LIZ) WILSON
YANÉ	CANDICE ORWELL
SACHÉ	SOFIA COPPOLA
SABÉ	KIERA KNIGHTLEY
REPUBLIC CRUISER CAPTAIN	BRONAGH GALLAGHER
REPUBLIC CRUISER PILOT	SILAS CARSON
TC-14	JOHN FENSOM
FODE	GREG PROOPS
BEED	SCOTT CAPURRO
JABBA THE HUTT	HIMSELF
JIRA	MARGARET TOWNER
KITSTER	DHRUV CHANCHANI
SEEK	OLIVER WALPOLE
AMEE	JENNA GREEN
MELEE	MEGAN UDALL
EETH KOTH	HASSANI SHAPI
ADI GALLIA	GIN
SAESEE TIIN	KHAN BONFILS
PLO KOON	ALAN RUSCOE
YARAEL POOF	MICHELLE TAYLOR
KI-ADI-MUNDI	SILAS CARSON
EVEN PIELL	MICHAELA COTTRELL
OPPO RANCISIS	JEROME BLAKE
DEPA BILLABA	DIPIKA O'NEILL JOTI
YADDLE	PHIL EASON
MAS AMEDDA	JEROME BLAKE
AKS MOE	MARK COULIER
LOTT DOD	SILAS CARSON
YODA PUPPETEERS	KATHY SMEE
	DON AUSTEN, DAVID GREENAWAY
VOICE OF TC-14	LINDSAY DUNCAN
VOICE OF DARTH MAUL	PETER SERAFINOWICZ
VOICE OF RUNE HAAKO	JAMES TAYLOR
VOICE OF DAULTAY DOFINE	CHRIS SANDERS
VOICE OF LOTT DOD	TOBY LONGWORTH
VOICE OF AKS MOE	MARC SILK
VOICE OF TEY HOW	TYGER

STUNT COORDINATOR/SWORDMASTER . . . . . NICK GILLARD

ASST STUNT COORDINATOR/STUNT DOUBLE . . . .
ANDREAS PETRIDES
STUNT PERFORMER/QUI-GON DOUBLE . . . . ROB INCH
STUNT PERFORMERS . . . . DOMINIC PREECE
RAY DE-HAAN, MORGAN JOHNSON, MARK NEWMAN
JOSS GOWER, DANNI BIERNAT

SUPERVISING ART DIRECTOR	PETER RUSSELL
ART DIRECTORS	FRED HOLE
	JOHN KING, ROD McLEAN, PHIL HARVEY
ART DIRECTOR (TUNISIA)	BEN SCOTT
DRAUGHTSMEN	PAUL CROSS
	NEIL MORFITT, GARY TOMKINS, TOAD TOZER
	JULIE PHILPOTT, JANE CLARK PEARCE
	PHILIP ELTON, MIKE BISHOP, LUCY RICHARDSON
SCENIC ARTIST	JAMES GEMMILL
UK CONCEPT ARTISTS	TONY WRIGHT
	KUN CHANG
UK ART DEPARTMENT COORDINATOR	LAURA BURROWS
JUNIOR DRAUGHTSMEN	HELEN XENOPOULOS
	REMO TOZZI
SCULPTORS	EDDIE BUTLER
	TESSA HARRISON, RICHARD MILLS, KEITH SHORT
	RICHARD SMITH
US CONCEPT ARTISTS	IAIN McCAIG
	TERRYL WHITLATCH, JAY SHUSTER, KURT KAUFMAN
	MARC GABBANA
STORYBOARD ARTIST	BENTON JEW
CONCEPT SCULPTORS	TONY McVEY
	MARK SIEGEL, ROBERT BARNES
CONCEPT MODEL MAKERS	JOHN GOODSON
	JOHN DUNCAN, ELLEN LEE
3-D COMPUTER MODELLERS	CAINE DICKINSON
	SIMON DUNSDON
US ART DEPARTMENT COORDINATORS	JILL JURKOWITZ
	BLAKE TUCKER
US ART DEPARTMENT ASSISTANT	TOM BARRATT
UK ART DEPARTMENT ASSISTANTS	
	CHRISTOPHER CHALLONER
	IAIN McFADYEN, CLAIRE NIA RICHARDS, EMMA TAUBER
CONCEPTUAL RESEARCHERS	JONATHAN BRESMAN
	DAVID CRAIG, KOICHI KURISU

PRE-VISUALIZATION/EFFECTS SUPERVISOR . . DAVID DOZORETZ

PRE-VISUALIZATION/EFFECTS ARTISTS . . EVAN PONTORIERO
RYAN TUDHOPE, KEVIN BAILLIE, JEFF WOZNIAK

PRODUCTION MANAGER	JO BURN
PRODUCTION MANAGER (TUNISIA)	PETER HESLOP
UNIT MANAGER (TUNISIA)	JEREMY JOHNS
SCRIPT SUPERVISOR	JAYNE-ANN TENGGREN
ASSISTANT TO RICK McCALLUM (UK)	ISOBEL THOMAS
ASSISTANTS TO RICK McCALLUM (US)	JANET NIELSEN
	SOPHIE MILTON
EXECUTIVE ASSISTANT TO GEORGE LUCAS	JANE BAY
SECRETARY TO GEORGE LUCAS	ANNE MERRIFIELD

PRODUCTION COORDINATORS . . . . .LISA PARKER
           HERMIONE NINNIM
PRODUCTION COORDINATOR (TUNISIA) . . . . .TORI PARRY
PRODUCTION COORDINATOR (ITALY) . . . .WINNIE WISHART
PRODUCTION COORDINATOR (TRAVEL) . . . . . . .MEL CLAUS
ASSISTANT PRODUCTION COORDINATOR . . . . .LEO MARTIN
UNIT NURSE . . . . .JEANIE UDALL
LOCATION MANAGERS . . . . .ROBERT JORDAN
           RICHARD SHARKEY
EXTRAS CASTING . . . . .SALLY MILLSON
CASTING ASSISTANT . . . . .KIRSTEN HAMPTON
ARTISTS' ASSISTANTS . . . . .KATE JONES
           JEMMA KEARNEY
CROWD ASSISTANT DIRECTOR . . . . .PAUL HIGGINS
FLOOR RUNNERS . . . . .TAMANA BLEASDALE
           NATHAN HOLMES
STUDIO RUNNERS . . . . .MELISSA LEIGH
      HENRY FORSYTH, JOE HALFORD, MARC WILTON
           MARTIN BROWN
PRODUCTION NETWORK ENGINEER . . . . . . .PAUL MATWIY
FIRE SAFETY OFFICER . . . . .DAVID DEANE

PRODUCTION CONTROLLER . . . . .KATHRYN FARRAR
PRODUCTION ACCOUNTANT . . . . .MICHELE TANDY
SET COST ACCOUNTANT . . . . .BETTY WILLIAMS
ACCOUNTING MANAGER . . . . .WENDY GORMAN
LOCATION ACCOUNTANT (TUNISIA) . . . . .DEAN HOOD
LOCATION ACCOUNTANT (ITALY) . . . . . .VAL SUNDERLAND
ASSISTANT ACCOUNTANT (TUNISIA) . . . .CLARE PLUMMER
ASSISTANT ACCOUNTANTS . . . . .RAJESHREE PATEL
      PENELOPE POWELL, BARBARA HARLEY
ACCOUNTS ASSISTANT . . . . .JEAN SIMMONS
ACCOUNTS RUNNER . . . . .SARAH-JANE WHEALE
ASSISTANT TO CONTROLLER . . . .ARDEES RABANG JUNDIS

CAMERA OPERATOR . . . . .TREVOR COOP
AERIAL CAMERAMAN . . . . .ADAM DALE
HELICOPTER PILOT . . . . .MARK WOLFE
FOCUS PULLERS . . . . .GRAHAM HALL
           BEN BUTLER
CLAPPER/LOADERS . . . . .JASON COOP
           SHAUN EVANS
STEADICAM OPERATOR . . . . .KEITH SEWELL
KEY GRIP . . . . .PETER MYSLOWSKI
SOUND RECORDIST . . . . .JOHN MIDGLEY
BOOM OPERATOR . . . . .JUNE PRINZ
SOUND ASSISTANT . . . . .CRAIG BURNS
LOCATION MATCHMOVE SUPERVISOR . . . . .JACK HAYE
MATCHMOVER . . . . .EDWARD COTTON
VIDEO PLAYBACK . . . . .LESTER DUNTON

           ANDREW HADDOCK
VIDEO PLAYBACK ASSISTANT . . .DATHI SVEINBJARNARSON
EFFECTS VIDEO ENGINEER . . . . .CLARK HIGGINS

SET DECORATOR . . . . .PETER WALPOLE
ASSISTANT SET DECORATOR . . . . . . .AMANDA BERNSTEIN
PRODUCTION BUYER . . . . .DEBORAH STOKELY
SUPERVISING DRESSING PROPMAN . . . .MARTIN KINGSLEY
CHARGEHAND DRESSING PROPMEN . . . . . .PETER WATSON
           KEITH PITT
DRESSING PROPMEN . . . . .BRIAN ALDRIDGE
PROPERTY MASTER . . . . .TY TEIGER
CHARGEHAND PROPMAKER . . . . .OLIVER HODGE
SENIOR PROPMAKER . . . . .TOBY HAWKES
PROPMAKERS . . . . .HOWARD MUNFORD
      JOHN WELLER, PIERRE BOHANNA,
    JIM BARR, WESLEY PEPPIATT, BRUCE CHEESMAN
    NICK TURNBULL, PETER LOOBY, GRANT TARBOX
    TERRY TOOHILL, PAUL HEARN, MATTHEW FOSTER
     SANDER ELLERS, LEE REEDER, JEFF KNIGHT
PROP STOREMAN . . . . .JONATHAN HURST
DRAPESMEN . . . . .COLIN FOX
           FRANK HOWE
SUPERVISING STAND-BY PROPMAN . . . . .BERNARD HEARN
STAND-BY PROPMAN . . . . .DANIEL HEARN

ASSISTANT COSTUME DESIGNER . . . . .ANN MASKREY
WARDROBE SUPERVISOR . . . . .SHARON LONG
CROWD PRE-FIT SUPERVISOR . . . . .SARAH JANE TOUAIBI
WARDROBE MASTER . . . . .ANTHONY BROOKMAN
WARDROBE MISTRESS . . . . .LOU DURKIN
WARDROBE ASSISTANTS . . . . .HELEN MATTOCKS
      NEIL MURPHY, NATALIE RODGERS
COSTUME PAINTERS . . . . .JOHN COWELL
           STEVEN GELL
TEXTILE ASSISTANTS . . . . .MARTIN MᶜSHANE
           EMMA WALKER
COSTUME PROPS ASSISTANTS . . . . .REUBEN HART
           PETER THOMPSON
COSTUME ACCESSORIES . . . . .KAREN SHANNON
           EMMA FRYER
COSTUME RUNNERS . . . . .KARN WEBSTER
           AMBER SMIT
COSTUME WORKROOM SUPERVISOR . . . . . .NICOLE YOUNG
COSTUME ASSISTANT . . . . .MICHAEL MOONEY
CUTTERS . . . . .KAY COVENEY
      SHARON MᶜCORMACK, DEBBIE MARCHANT
COSTUME PROPS MODELLER . . . . .IVO COVENEY
WORKROOM ASSISTANTS . . . . .ANNE MATHESON
      MARNIE ORMISTON, ARABELLA DEAN

PAUL SHARPE
LINDA SIEGEL
DOUGLAS J. SMITH
BRIAN SORBO
CHRISTA STARR
DAVID STEPHENS
CHRIS STILLMAN
JOHN STILLMAN
RUSS SUEYOSHI
CATHERINE TATE
TIM TERAMOTO
ERIC TEXIER
MARC TOSCANO
ALEX TROPIEC

HANS UHLIG
ERIC VOEGELS
JOHN WALKER
ANDY WANG
ROBERT WEAVER
SUSAN WEEKS
DAVID WEITZBERG
COLIE WERTZ
KEN WESLEY
MELVA YOUNG
DEAN YURKE
KEN ZIEGLER
RITA ZIMMERMAN

CHARACTER ANIMATORS

PHILIP ALEXY
CHRIS ARMSTRONG
PATRICK BONNEAU
SUSAN CAMPBELL
MARC CHU
CHI CHUNG TSE
KYLE CLARK
BRUCE DAHL
ANDREW DOUCETTE
ANDREW GRANT
PAUL GRIFFIN
KENT HAMMERSTROM
TIM HARRINGTON
JASON IVIMEY
SHAWN KELLY
KEN KING
STEVE LEE
MARTIN L'HEUREUX
VICTORIA LIVINGSTONE
KEVIN MARTEL

GLEN McINTOSH
NEIL MICHKA
CHRISTOPHER MINOS
CHRISTOPHER MITCHELL
JACQUES MULLER
JULIE NELSON
STEVE NICHOLS
DANA O'CONNOR
RICK O'CONNOR
DAVID PARSONS
STEVE RAWLINS
JAY RENNIE
MAGALI RIGAUDIAS
TRISH SCHUTZ
TOM ST. AMAND
GLENN SYLVESTER
SI TRAN
SCOTT WIRTZ
ANDY WONG
WILLIAM R. WRIGHT

DIGITAL MODEL DEVELOPMENT
AND CONSTRUCTION ARTISTS

STEPHEN APLIN
DONNA BEARD
DUGAN BEACH
SCOTT BONNENFANT
ROBERT BRUCE
KEN BRYAN
ANDREW CAWRSE
SIMON CHEUNG
CATHERINE CRAIG
AARON FERGUSON

PAUL GIACOPPO
DEREK GILLINGHAM
REBECCA HESKES
JEAN-CLAUDE LANGER
LENNY LEE
SUNNY LI-HSIEN WEI
ALYSON MARKELL
RUSSELL PAUL
AARON PFAU
COREY ROSEN

DAVID SACCHERI
TONY SOMMERS
HOWIE WEED

RON WOODALL
ELBERT YEN

DIGITAL MATTE ARTISTS

RONN BROWN
BRIAN FLORA
CAROLEEN GREEN
JONATHAN HARB
PAUL HUSTON

BILL MATHER
RICK RISCHE
MARK SULLIVAN
YUSEI UESUGI
WEI ZHENG

ROTOSCOPE/PAINT SUPERVISORS . .SUSAN KELLY-ANDREWS
JACK MONGOVAN
LEAD VISUAL EFFECTS COORDINATOR . . . . .LISA TODD
VISUAL EFFECTS PRODUCTION ACCOUNTANT
. . . . .JOSHUA MARKS
PROJECTIONIST . . . . .KENN MOYNIHAN
MOTION CAPTURE SUPERVISOR . . . . .JEFF LIGHT
DIGITAL COLOR TIMING SUPERVISORS . .BRUCE VECCHITTO
KENNETH SMITH
3D MATCHMOVE SUPERVISORS . . . . .KEITH JOHNSON
DAVID WASHBURN
RESEARCH & DEVELOPMENT SUPERVISOR . . . .
CHRISTIAN ROUET
ADDITIONAL MATTE PAINTINGS . . . . .BILL GEORGE

VISUAL EFFECTS EDITORS

SCOTT BALCEREK
DAVID TANAKA

GREG HYMAN
JOHN BARTLE

VISUAL EFFECTS COORDINATORS

ALEXANDRA ALTROCCHI
LORI ARNOLD
LIZ BROWN
MICHAELA CALANCHINI
DAVID DRANITZKE
VICKI ENGEL
MONIQUE GOUGEON
DAVID GRAY

SUSAN GREENHOW
AMANDA MONTGOMERY
LUKE O'BYRNE
CHRISTINE OWENS
PENNY RUNGE
ROBIN SAXEN
DAVID VALENTIN

DIGITAL ROTOSCOPE / PAINT ARTISTS

TRANG BACH
KATHARINE BAIRD
LANCE BAETKEY
CHRIS BAYZ
RENE BINKOWSKI
BETH D'AMATO
SCOTT DAVID
KATE ELSEN
KELLY FISCHER

DAWN GATES
SUSAN GOLDSMITH
CAM GRIFFIN
JIRI JACKNOWITZ
PATRICK JARVIS
REGAN MCGEE
KATIE MORRIS
AARON MUSZALSKI
ANDREW NELSON

ELSA RODRIGUEZ   JAMES VALENTINE
JOE SALAZAR   MIKE VAN EPS
ZACHARY SHERMAN   ERIN WEST
DAVID SULLIVAN

3D MATCHMOVE ARTISTS

ALIA AGHA   JOSEPH METTEN
JIM HAGEDORN   DANI MORROW
DAVID HANKS   MELISSA MULLIN
LUKE LONGIN   TALMAGE WATSON
DAVID MANOS MORRIS   R.D. WEGENER

MOTION CAPTURE GROUP

ALEXANDRE FRAZAO   SETH ROSENTHAL
DOUGLAS GRIFFIN   MICHAEL SANDERS
ANN McCOLGAN

VISUAL EFFECTS STORYBOARD / CONCEPTUAL ARTISTS

BRICE COX JR.   JULES MANN
WARREN FU   NOEL RUBIN

FILM SCANNING AND RECORDING

RANDALL BEAN   NANCY JENCKS
EARL BEYER   DOUG JONES
ANDREA BIKLIAN   JAMES LIM
MICHAEL CORDOVA   TODD MITCHELL
MICHAEL ELLIS   JOSH PINES
GEORGE GAMBETTA   STEPHANIE TAUBERT
TIM GEIDEMAN   ALAN TRAVIS
LYDIA GREENFIELD

VISUAL EFFECTS EDITORIAL STAFF

NIC ANASTASSIOU   IAN MCCAMEY
CAREY BURENS   JIM MILTON
EDWIN DUNKLEY   MIKE MORGAN
NATALEE DJOKOVIC   ELLEN SCHADE
DAWN MARTIN   ANTHONY PITONE

SOFTWARE DEVELOPMENT

JOHN ANDERSON   CARY PHILLIPS
DAVID BENSON   NICOLAS POPRAVKA
ROD BOGART   VISHWA RANJAN
TOMMY BURNETTE   ERIC SCHAFER
JOHN HORN   VINCENT TOSCANO
JIM HOURIHAN   ALAN TROMBLA
ZORAN KAãIã-ALESIã   JEFFERY YOST
FLORIAN KAINZ

VISUAL EFFECTS PRODUCTION AND TECHNICAL SUPPORT

NOEL BREVICK   JONATHAN LITT
SEAN CASEY   DANIEL LOBL
MEI MING CASINO   DANA MASINO
FAY DAVID   JENNIFER NONA
TOM FIRESTONE   MARISA PEARL
DOUGLAS APPLEWHITE   DAVID OWEN
CEDRICK CHAN   DON ROTTIERS
BRIAN GEE   MASAYORI OKA
KATHY GARDNER   KIM ORLA- BUKOWSKI
DIANA GAZDIK   MIKE PETERS
SAM GRANAT   MARC SADEGHI
KALEEM KARMAN   LESLIE SAFLEY
BRIAN KASPER   DAMIAN STEEL
TODD KRISH   BILL TLUSTY
BILL GRINDER   ANTHONY SHAFER
SEAN HOESSLI   MARC WILHITE
JOHN LEVIN   CARRIE WOLBERG
KIMBERLY LASHBROOK

DIGITAL OPERATIONS AND TECHNOLOGY GROUP

BRIAN BRECHT   JEFF KING
ENDLA BURROWS   DAN LEE
KIPP ALDRICH   NANCY LUCKOFF
KEN BEYER   KEN MARUYAMA
STEWART BIRNAM   RALEIGH MANN
GAIL CURREY   GARRICK MEEKER
VICKI DOBBS BECK   WILL MELICK
RUSSELL DARLING   CLIFF PLUMER
GREG DUNN   BETH SASSEEN
SCOTT GRENIER   GARY MEYER
SHANNON HENRY   FRED MEYERS
JAY JOHNSON   JOE TAKAI
MARY HINMAN

MINIATURE CONSTRUCTION AND PHOTOGRAPHY UNIT

MODEL SUPERVISOR
STEVE GAWLEY

CHIEF MODEL MAKERS

WILLIAM BECK   GIOVANNI DONOVAN
STEVE WALTON   KEITH LONDON
BARBARA AFFONSO   IRA KEELER
CHARLIE BAILEY   LORNE PETERSON
BRIAN GERNAND   MICHAEL LYNCH

MODEL MAKERS

LAUREN ABRAMS	VICTORIA LEWIS
CARL ASSMUS	TODD LOOKINLAND
CAROL BAUMAN	ALAN LYNCH
SALVATORE BELLECI	SCOTT McNAMARA
DON BIES	AMY MILLER
NICK BLAKE	RODNEY MORGAN
NICK BOGLE	WENDY MORTON
JEFF BREWER	DAVE MURPHY
PHIL BROTHERTON	RANDY OTTENBERG
MARK BUCK	ALAN PETERSON
NICK d'ABO	TONY PRECIADO
FON DAVIS	TOM PROOST
BRIAN DEWE	R. KIM SMITH
ROBERT EDWARDS	MICHAEL STEFFE
MARK FIORENZA	EBEN STROMQUIST
DAVID FOGLER	LARRY TAN
JON FOREMAN	TREVOR TUTTLE
CHRIS GOEHE	LAUREN VOGT
JON GUIDINGER	DANNY WAGNER
PEGGY HRASTAR	MARK WALAS
AARON HAYE	MELANIE WALAS
GRANT IMAHARA	KEVIN WALLACE
ERIK JENSEN	CHUCK WILEY
MICHAEL JOBE	JULIE WOODBRIDGE
KELLY LEPKOWSKI	ERAN YACHDAV

EFFECTS DIRECTORS OF PHOTOGRAPHY . . . .
MARTY ROSENBERG
PATRICK SWEENEY, PAT TURNER, RAY GILBERTI
CAMERA OPERATORS . . . . .CARL MILLER
VANCE PIPER
ASSISTANT CAMERA OPERATORS . . . . .BOB HILL
JOHN GAZDIK, MICHAEL BIENSTOCK
GAFFERS . . . . .MICHAEL OLAGUE
TIM MORGAN
KEY GRIPS . . . . .BILL BARR
BERNIE DEMOLSKI
CHIEF COSTUMER . . . . .ANNIE POLLAND
CAMERA ENGINEERING . . . . .GREG BEAUMONTE
MIKE MACKENZIE, DUNCAN SUTHERLAND
STAGE COORDINATOR . . . . .MEGAN CARLSON

GRIP AND ELECTRIC CREW

JOE ALLEN	CRAIG MOHAGEN
TOM CLOUTIER	CHUCK RAY
RON DIGGORY	JOHN SILER
DENNIS GEHRINGER	DAVE WATSON
DANNY MICHALSKE	

SPECIAL EFFECTS PYROTECHNICS CREW

SPECIAL EFFECTS SUPERVISOR . . . . .GEOFF HERON
SPECIAL EFFECTS BEST BOY . . . . .ROBBIE CLOT
SPECIAL EFFECTS TECHNICIAN . . . . .DAVE HERON
DATA CAPTURE SYSTEM SUPPLIED BY . . . .
ARRI MEDIA, MUNICH
VISUAL EFFECTS PROCESSING & PRINTS BY . . . .
MONACO LABORATORIES, SAN FRANCISCO

POST PRODUCTION SOUND SERVICES PROVIDED BY
SKYWALKER SOUND
A DIVISION OF LUCAS DIGITAL LTD. LLC ,
MARIN COUNTY, CALIFORNIA

RE-RECORDING MIXERS . . . . .GARY RYDSTROM
TOM JOHNSON, SHAWN MURPHY
ADR RECORDIST . . . . .MATTHEW WOOD
ADR RECORDED AT . . . . .COMPASS POINT STUDIOS,
NASSAU, BAHAMAS, MAGMASTERS
FOLEY MIXER . . . . .TONY ECKERT
FOLEY RECORDIST . . . . .FRANK 'PEPE' MEREL
SUPERVISING SOUND EDITORS . . . . .BEN BURTT
TOM BELLFORT
CO-SUPERVISING SOUND EDITOR . . . . . .MATTHEW WOOD
SOUND EFFECTS EDITORS . . . . .TERESA ECKTON
CHRIS SCARABOSIO
DIALOGUE/ADR EDITORS . . . . .SARA BOLDER
GWENDOLYN YATES WHITTLE
FOLEY EDITORS . . . . .BRUCE LACEY
MARIAN WILDE
FOLEY ARTISTS . . . . .DENNIE THORPE
JANA VANCE
RE-RECORDIST . . . . .RONALD G. ROUMAS
MIX TECHNICIANS . . . . .TONY SERENO
JURGEN SCHARPF, KENT SPARLING
MACHINE ROOM OPERATORS . . . . . . .BRANDON PROCTOR
STEPHEN ROMANKO, JENNIFER BARIN
ASSISTANT SOUND EDITORS . . . . .KEVIN SELLERS
STEVE SLANEC
ASSISTANT DIALOGUE/ADR EDITOR . . .JESSICA BELLFORT
DIGITAL AUDIO TRANSFER SUPERVISOR . . . .
JONATHAN GREBER
DIGITAL AUDIO TRANSFER . . . . .DEE SELBY
CHRISTOPHER BARRON
VIDEO SERVICES . . . . .CHRISTIAN VON BURKLEO
JOHN TORRIJOS
PROJECTIONIST . . . . .SCOTT BREWER
MUSIC EDITOR . . . . .KEN WANNBERG
ASSISTANT MUSIC EDITOR . . . . .PETER MYLES
ORCHESTRATIONS . . . . .JOHN NEUFELD
CONRAD POPE

MUSIC RECORDED AT . . . . .ABBEY ROAD STUDIOS
SCORING ENGINEER . . . . .SHAWN MURPHY
SCORING ASSISTANTS . . . . .JONATHAN ALLEN
ANDREW DUDMAN
MUSIC PREPARATION . . . . .DAKOTA MUSIC SERVICE
JO ANN KANE MUSIC SERVICE
MUSIC PERFORMED BY . .LONDON SYMPHONY ORCHESTRA

ORCHESTRA LEADER . . . . .GORDAN NIKOLITCH
CHOIRS .LONDON VOICES
NEW LONDON CHILDREN'S CHOIR
CHORUS DIRECTORS . . . . .TERRY EDWARDS
RONALD CORP

DIRECTOR OF PUBLICITY . . . . .LYNNE HALE
UNIT PUBLICIST . . . . .KATE CAMPBELL
CHIEF STILLS PHOTOGRAPHER . . . . . . .KEITH HAMSHERE
STILLS PHOTOGRAPHERS . . . . .GILES KEYTE
JONATHAN FISHER
PHOTOGRAPHY ASSISTANT . . . . .DEREK BOYES
STILLS PROCESSING BY . . . . .PINEWOOD STUDIOS
DOCUMENTARY CINEMATOGRAPHER . . . .JONATHAN SHENK
DOCUMENTARY SOUND RECORDISTS . . . . . .MARK BECKER
GUY HAKE
IMAGE ARCHIVIST . . . . .TINA MILLS
RESEARCHERS . . . . .JO DONALDSON
CHERYL EDWARDS, JENNY CRAIK

SECOND UNIT
SECOND UNIT DIRECTOR . . . . .ROGER CHRISTIAN
DIRECTOR OF PHOTOGRAPHY . . . . .GILES NUTTGENS
FIRST ASSISTANT DIRECTOR . . . . .NICK HECKSTALL-SMITH
SECOND ASSISTANT DIRECTOR . . . . . . .GEORGE WALKER
THIRD ASSISTANT DIRECTOR . . . . .JANET NIELSEN
SCRIPT SUPERVISOR . . . . .LISA VICK
FOCUS PULLER . . . . .STEVEN HALL
CLAPPER LOADERS . . . . .EDWARD MEREDYDD JONES
IAN COFFEY
GRIP . . . . .MARK BINNALL
WARDROBE ASSISTANTS . . . . .DAY MURCH
JANE PETRIE, NIGEL EGERTON
ART DIRECTOR . . . . .RICKY EYRES
GAFFER .DAVID SMITH
CHARGEHAND STAND-BY PROPMAN . . . . . .PAUL TURNER
STAND-BY PROPMAN . . . . .ROBERT THORNE
STAND-BY CARPENTER . . . . .PAUL NOTT-MACAIRE
STAND-BY RIGGER . . . . .STEVE SANSOM JR
MAKE-UP ARTIST . . . . .TREFOR PROUD
HAIRDRESSER . . . . .HILARY HAINES
MATCHMOVER . . . . .CATRIN MEREDYDD
VIDEO PLAYBACK . . . . .LUCIEN NUNES VAZ

BEST BOY .DAVE RIDOUT
ELECTRICIANS . . . . .SONNY BURDIS
RICHARD OXLEY

STAND-IN FOR LIAM NEESON . . . . .GAVIN HALE
STAND-IN FOR EWAN McGREGOR . . . . . . .STEVE RICARD
STAND-IN FOR NATALIE PORTMAN . . . . .JOAN FIELD
STAND-IN FOR JAKE LLOYD . . . . . . .RAYMOND GRIFFITHS
UTILITY STAND-INS . . . . .PAUL KITE
CHRISTIAN SIMPSON

SPECIAL EFFECTS SUPERVISOR . . . . . .PETER HUTCHINSON
SENIOR SPECIAL EFFECTS TECHNICIANS . . . .TERRY GLASS
DIGBY BETTISON-MILNER, ANTHONY PHELAN
LES WHEELER, ANDY BUNCE
SPECIAL EFFECTS COORDINATOR . . .BRENDA HUTCHINSON
R2-D2 OPERATOR . . . . .JOLYON BAMBRIDGE
SPECIAL EFFECTS TECHNICIANS . . . . .JIM CROCKETT
STEPHEN HUTCHINSON, BARRY ANGUS
MARK HOWARD, SEAN McCONVILLE, GRAHAM RIDDELL

TUNISIA SHOOT
PRODUCTION SERVICES PROVIDED BY
CTV SERVICES, TUNIS, TUNISIA

PRODUCTION SUPERVISOR . . . . .ABDELAZIZ BEN MLOUKA
UNIT MANAGERS . . . . .MEIMOUN MAHBOULI
PHILIPPA DAY
PRODUCTION COORDINATOR . . . . .AMEL BECHARNIA
LOCATION MANAGER . . . . .MOSLAH KRAIEM
TRANSPORT MANAGER . . . . .LASSAAD MEJRI
PRODUCTION ACCOUNTANT . . . . . . .ABDALLAH BALOUCHE
ART DIRECTOR . . . . .TAIEB JALLOULI
1ST ASSISTANT DIRECTOR . . . . .MOEZ KAMOUN
PROP MASTER/BUYER . . . . .MOHAMED BARGAOUI
GRIP . . . . .HASSEN TEBBI
GAFFER . . . . .LOTFI SIALA
MAKE-UP ASSISTANT . . . . .HAGER BOUHAOUALA
WARDROBE SUPERVISOR . . . . .NAAMA JAZI MEJRI

ITALY SHOOT
PRODUCTION SERVICES PROVIDED BY
MESTIERE CINEMA, VENICE, ITALY

PRODUCTION SUPERVISOR . . . . .GUIDO CERASUOLO
UNIT MANAGER . . . . .ENRICO BALLARIN
PRODUCTION COORDINATOR . . . . .LAURA CAPPATO
LOCATION MANAGER . . . . .FRANCO RAPA
LOCATION ASSISTANT . . . . .UGO CRISCUOLO
ART DIRECTOR . . . . .LIVIA BORGOGNONI

PRODUCTION ASSISTANT . . . . .NICOLA ROSADA
FIRST ASSISTANT DIRECTOR . . . . .DAVID TURCHI
SECOND ASSISTANT DIRECTOR . . . . .DARIO CIONI
THIRD ASSISTANT DIRECTOR . . . . .ANDREA BONI
TRANSPORT CAPTAIN . . . . .FABIO MANCINI
ACCOUNTANT . . . . .CARLA ZACCHIA
PAYROLL . . . . .MARILENA LA FERRARA
CASHIER .CLAUDIA BRAVIN

TRANSPORT CAPTAIN . . . . .PHIL ALLCHIN

UNIT DRIVERS

GEORGE ANDREWS	JOHN HOLLYWOOD
BRIAN ESTERBROOK	PETER COLLINS
NIGEL BIRTCHNELL	CHRIS STREETER
PETER GRAOVAC	MARK DAVIES
GARRY CLARK	STEVE TIMMS

CATERING BY . . . . .HOLLYWOOD CATERING SERVICES
CATERING MANAGER . . . . .TIM DE'ATH
ARTISTES' CHEF . . . . .MARK REYNOLDS
CRAFT SERVICE . . . . .SOPHIE MELLOR

SPECIAL THANKS TO:
JIM MORRIS
GLORIA BORDERS
PATRICIA BLAU
STEVE SMITH
SIMON TAY
DANIEL DARK
SALLY BULLOCK
CHAPEAU ATELIER
RUNCO VIDEO INTERNATIONAL
PARASOUND-HOME THEATER
DON POST
ANNA BIES
FRAMESTORE, LONDON
MAXXIOM LIMITED
GALLERY SOFTWARE
TUNIS AIR
PEOPLE OF TOZEUR, TATAOUINE & MEDENINE, TUNISIA
TUNISIAN MINISTRY OF THE INTERIOR
ITALIAN MINISTRY OF ART AND CULTURE
SUPERINTENDENT OF THE HERITAGE OF CASERTA & BEN-
EVENTO
ITALIAN AIR FORCE TRAINING SCHOOL FOR NONCOMMIS-
SIONED OFFICERS
GOVERNOR AND CITY OF CASERTA
POLICE & CARABINIERI OF CASERTA
ITALIAN AIR FORCE - AIRFIELD CAPODICHINO, NAPLES

HERTS FILM LINK
HEVER CASTLE
BRITISH MUSICIANS UNION
AZTEC MODELS
ELECTROHOME PROJECTION SYSTEMS
DOREMI LABS, INC
SONY CORPORATION OF AMERICA
APPLE COMPUTERS

FILMED AT LEAVESDEN STUDIOS, LEAVESDEN, ENGLAND
AND ON LOCATION IN CASERTA, ITALY AND TOZEUR, MEDE-
NINE & TATAOUINE, TUNISIA

MIXED & RECORDED IN A THX CERTIFIED FACILITY

COLOR BY RANK (DELUXE) FILM LABORATORIES, UK
PRINTS BY DELUXE LABORATORIES
DAILIES TELECINE BY MIDNIGHT TRANSFER, LONDON
FILM EDITED ON AVID FILM COMPOSERS
END CREDITS BY PACIFIC TITLE
NEGATIVE CUTTING BY KONA CUTTING
PRODUCTION VEHICLES BY MICKY WEBB TRANSPORT
PRODUCTION SPEAKER SYSTEMS BY M & K SOUND
LOCATION PROJECTION FACILITIES BY DIGITAL PROJECTION
WESCAM CAMERA BY FLYING PICTURES UK LTD
UNDERWATER TANK BY ACTION UNDERWATER STUDIOS LTD
SCRIPTS BY SAPEX SCRIPTS
COMMUNICATIONS EQUIPMENT BY WAVEVEND LTD
PRODUCTION LEGAL SERVICES BY . . . .
                BILLY HINSHELWOOD-MARRIOTT HARRISON
INSURANCE SERVICES BY . . . .
                DAVID HAVARD–AON/ALBERT G RUBEN
EUROPEAN TRAVEL SERVICES BY . . . .
                SUE ROBERTS-THE TRAVEL COMPANY
US TRAVEL SERVICES BY . . . .
                CATHY NILSEN-DIRECT ACCESS
UK SHIPPING SERVICES BY . . .DYNAMIC INTERNATIONAL
                FREIGHT SERVICES
US SHIPPING SERVICES BY . . . . .INTERNATIONAL
                CARGO SERVICES
ON-LINE & TELECINE SERVICES BY . . . .WESTERN IMAGES,
                SAN FRANCISCO
ELECTRIC IMAGE 3D SOFTWARE BY . . . . .PLAY INC.
COMPUTERS BY . . . . .SILICON GRAPHICS
COMMOTION VISUAL EFFECTS SOFTWARE BY . . . .
                PUFFIN DESIGNS
DIGITAL STORAGE BY . . . .HAMMER STORAGE SOLUTIONS
PRODUCTION SOFTWARE BY . .COLUMBUS ENTERTAINMENT
DE-HISS PROCESSING BY . . . . .CEDAR DH-1,
                HHB COMMUNICATIONS INC.

LIGHTING EQUIPMENT BY   . .AFM LIGHTING LTD, LONDON

ARRIFLEX CAMERA & HAWK ANAMORPHIC LENSES
SUPPLIED BY .ARRI MEDIA
SHOT ON KODAK MOTION PICTURE FILM

SOUNDTRACK AVAILABLE ON SONY CLASSICAL
READ THE NOVEL FROM DEL REY BOOKS

DOLBY DIGITAL IN SELECTED THEATRES
SONY DYNAMIC DIGITAL SOUND IN SELECTED THEATRES

DTS DIGITAL SOUND IN SELECTED THEATRES

APPROVED NO. xxxxx
MOTION PICTURE ASSOCIATION OF AMERICA

THE EVENTS, CHARACTERS AND FIRMS DEPICTED IN
THIS PHOTOPLAY ARE FICTITIOUS. ANY SIMILARITY TO

ACTUAL PERSONS, LIVING OR DEAD, OR TO ACTUAL
EVENTS OR FIRMS IS PURELY COINCIDENTAL

OWNERSHIP OF THIS MOTION PICTURE IS PROTECTED BY
COPYRIGHT AND OTHER APPLICABLE LAWS, AND ANY
UNAUTHORIZED DUPLICATION, DISTRIBUTION OR
EXHIBITION OF THIS MOTION PICTURE COULD RESULT IN
CRIMINAL PROSECUTION AS WELL AS CIVIL LIABILITY.

COPYRIGHT © 1999 LUCASFILM LTD
ALL RIGHTS RESERVED

RELEASED BY TWENTIETH CENTURY FOX FILM
CORPORATION

THIS FILM HAS BEEN RATED xxxx

QUALITY ASSURANCE SERVICES WERE PROVIDED BY THE
THX THEATRE ALIGNMENT PROGRAM

EVERY SAGA HAS A BEGINNING

STAR WARS

EPISODE I

THE PHANTOM MENACE™

STAR WARS   EPISODE I   THE PHANTOM MENACE
Starring LIAM NEESON   EWAN McGREGOR   NATALIE PORTMAN   JAKE LLOYD   IAN McDIARMID
Co-starring ANTHONY DANIELS   KENNY BAKER   PERNILLA AUGUST   FRANK OZ
Music by JOHN WILLIAMS   Produced by RICK McCALLUM
Written and Directed by
GEORGE LUCAS

   Special Visual Effects and Animation by INDUSTRIAL LIGHT & MAGIC
A LUCASFILM LTD. Production – A TWENTIETH CENTURY FOX Release
Soundtrack Available on SONY CLASSICAL Read the Novel from DEL REY BOOKS
w w w . s t a r w a r s . c o m

About the Authors

Laurent Bouzereau is the author of *The De Palma Cut, The Alfred Hitchcock Quote Book, The Cutting Room Floor, Ultraviolent Movies, and Star Wars: The Annotated Screenplays.* Bouzereau has written, directed, and produced recent documentaries on the making of Steven Spielberg's *Jaws, Close Encounters of the Third Kind, 1941, E.T. the Extra-Terrestrial*, and *The Lost World: Jurassic Park*; George Lucas's *American Graffiti*; Brian De Palma's *Scarface*; Francis Ford Coppola's *The Godfather* Trilogy; Alfred Hitchcock's *Psycho*; Martin Scorcese's *Taxi Driver;* and Lawrence Kasdan's *The Big Chill* and *Silverado*.

Jody Duncan has authored dozens of articles on motion picture technology for *Cinefex* magazine, and has served as that publication's editor since 1992. She is also the author of many books on the making of major motion pictures, including *The Making of The X-Files movie, The Making of The Lost World: Jurassic Park, The Making of Jurassic Park*, and *The Making of Terminator 2: Judgment Day*. Her play, *A Warring Absence*, won a national playwriting award, and was produced in Los Angeles in 1994.